*Dear M_*
May you be
*for the hours y_*
with love
Helen xx

CW00540592

Be Fruitful

A 40-day devotional journey
into greater fruitfulness

Helen Roberts

RIVER
PUBLISHING

River Publishing & Media Ltd
Bradbourne Stables
East Malling
Kent
ME19 6DZ
United Kingdom

info@river-publishing.co.uk

MIX
Paper from
responsible sources
FSC® C117931

ISBN 978-1-908393-70-8
Cover design by www.spiffingcovers.com
Printed & bound by MBM Print SCS Ltd, Glasgow

CONTENTS

Dedication   05
Acknowledgements   06
Introduction   07

Section 1: Remain Rooted in the *Who* Not the *What*

Day 1 –   By Divine Design   11
Day 2 –   Spiritually Saturated   16
Day 3 –   Commit Completely   20
Day 4 –   Delight in the Who   25
Day 5 –   The Posture of Permission   29
Day 6 –   Habits for Harvest   34
Day 7 –   Distinctly Distinct   39
Day 8 –   Never Neglect   43
Day 9 –   Partnering for Fruitfulness   48
Day 10 – Waiting With Hope   53
Day 11 – Hidden Treasures   58
Day 12 – Seeds and Soils   63
Day 13 – Growing in the Dark   68

Section 2: Knowing the Gardener

Day 14 – Who Holds the Secateurs?   74
Day 15 – Stirring in Stuff   78
Day 16 – Dormant Potential   83
Day 17 – Him First   87
Day 18 – Less For More   91
Day 19 – Fruitful Attitudes   95
Day 20 – Alien Invasion   100
Day 21 – Significant Roots for Big Fruits   105
Day 22 – With Added Loss   109
Day 23 – Ask Again   114
Day 24 – His Fingerprints are Over You   119
Day 25 – In the "Horribilis"   124
Day 26 – A-Mazing Growth   129

Section 3: Expect More

Day 27 – Seasons   134
Day 28 – No Limits   138
Day 29 – The Greatest of These Is...   142
Day 30 – Real Strength   147
Day 31 – Peace   151
Day 32 – Altitude, Attitude and Aptitude   156
Day 33 – A.R.K.   161
Day 34 – Pursued   166
Day 35 – Forever and Ever   171
Day 36 – Strongly Gentle   176
Day 37 – Marshmallow Moments   180
Day 38 – Evergreen   184
Day 39 – Standing Back   189
Day 40 – Expect More   194

About the Author   199

DEDICATION

———•———

To David Ollerton.

I will be forever grateful for such an incredible spiritual father during my foundational years of faith – one who was always there for me and continually planted spiritual seeds in my life that would grow into a passionate love for the Word of God. May the fruit from your life have many seeds in it and produce many generations of disciples, equally passionate for God's Word and Spirit – even through these pages. Thank you for running your earthly race well, to the very end. You will be missed, but your life leaves a legacy.

ACKNOWLEDGEMENTS

This book is a team effort in so many ways and I am grateful to every team member who has made it what it is. Yet with particular thanks:

To my hub, Tim – thank you for still loving me so wholeheartedly and for championing me to be the best version of me. Thank you for not fainting when I said there was another book-baby on the way. Thank you for knowing more about punctuation than I do and for graciously encouraging me to grow! I love you completely. You are my most favourite person on the planet!

To Bethany, Hannah and David – my three most favourite children. Thank you for giving me space when I needed to write, whilst not letting me forget there are humans in my home to share life with.

To all the Staff Team and Senior Leadership Team of Wellspring Church – thank you for continuing to encourage me to persevere in taking hold of that for which Christ has taken hold of me.

To Nikki W – thank you for encouraging me to keep my priorities in order and for sharing the journey. Thank you for doing so much to make it possible for me to be released to write. You are a treasured friend.

To Cathy D – thank you for your eye for detail, for correcting my mistakes so graciously and for being such an essential part of this book-baby-team! Your care grows my confidence.

To the whole family of Wellspring Church – it is my privilege to journey with you – you are the best family ever!

To Tim Pettingale – thank you for believing in me again, risking your reputation on me again and for being an amazing "midwife" to this next book-baby. Thank you for your encouragement along the way – even for the "brutal" feedback at times. You and your team at River Publishing are incredible.

Thank you to everyone who read *Be Victorious*, gave me feedback, wrote reviews and encouraged me to write again. May you all remain victorious and be wonderfully fruitful for the Lord's glory.

Be Fruitful

INTRODUCTION

Over the next forty days we are going to go on a journey together, to explore what it means to live a life that is really fruitful. We'll learn together how this can happen. Jesus told His disciples how they could be fruitful if they remained in Him (John 15, which we will examine later). In addition He also told them that they could be even more fruitful if they trusted His Father – the Gardener – and allowed Him to prune them. For us, as for the first disciples, this means removing anything that isn't bearing fruit in order to see an increased harvest from that which is fruitful.

So, we are going to consider what it is to remain in Christ. How can we let the Gardener do what He does best? What fruit can our lives really produce?

Reading the Word of God every day is a life-giving discipline, so if you've already established this habit then I pray this book will bring you a refreshing, deepening encounter with the Father. If you are seeking to establish a new habit of exploring the Word every day, then I pray you will persevere and enjoy this encounter. The Father longs to meet with you.

Every day there is a verse or two to meditate on. It may help to write it out on a post-it note and put it somewhere prominent, or post it on a social media platform. Let this verse become part of your day and fill you with truth.

I encourage you to share this journey with a friend. Even if you read in private, perhaps you can chat about what you've read with a friend. Each day's entry ends with an opportunity to question how you can go deeper still. These questions will help you even more if you share them with a friend, accountability partner, in a small group, or in an online discussion.

It can really help to have a specific place set aside as your space for reading each day. Keep a Bible there, along with a journal, this devotional and a pen. Get everything ready, so that you're not wasting time rooting out what you need, but instead are digging deeper into the Word!

Finally, before putting this book down each day, pause and pray. Invite the Holy Spirit to confirm in you what He wants to say. Invite the Holy Spirit to allow the truths to take root in your heart. Expect fruit to come from each day.

Thank you for starting this journey. I am cheering you on all the way. Make up your mind to finish what is starting here today.

Bless you heaps,
Helen.

Section 1

---•---

REMAIN ROOTED IN THE *WHO* NOT THE *WHAT*

DAY 1:
BY DIVINE DESIGN

——·——

*"Oh, that my actions would consistently reflect your decrees!
Then I will not be ashamed when I compare my life with your
commands."*
(Psalm 119:5-6)

In all things, except possibly our waistlines, most of us want to grow. Whether it's in our relationships, finances, health or any other area, we all want to see our lives being productive.

Healthy things grow. Even the smallest of living cells, if healthy, will multiply and grow; expand and thrive. Growth and productivity are both eagerly desired and celebrated by many in a variety of circumstances. Proud parents mark the milestones in their children's lives, notching their increasing height on the doorpost. They put their children's certificates on the wall, celebrating growth. Students celebrate their educational growth when they complete their courses. People celebrate the work promotions that enable their bank accounts to grow (no doubt to pay for their growing child's new shoes or student fees!)

Children often long to grow in height, or popularity. A footballer wants to grow in skill. An entrepreneur wants to grow new opportunities. A leader wants to grow in influence. Most of us want our lives to be growing in both purpose and fruitfulness. Few, if any, of us would admit to wanting less money, fewer loved ones or less purpose in our life. Even though we may express our gratitude for the fruitfulness we've already experienced, we are still open to "more".

Jesus told His disciples,

"Remain in me, and I will remain in you. For a branch cannot produce fruit if it is severed from the vine, and you cannot be fruitful unless you remain in me." (John 15:4)

He went on to tell them that,

"When you produce much fruit, you are my true disciples. This brings great glory to my Father." (John 15:8)

Fruitfulness, according to Jesus, is both a sign and a result. It's a sign of our follower-ship of Him and a result of us remaining in Him. On this devotional journey we are going to start by exploring what it is to remain in Jesus.

The Creation narrative tells us that, before speaking life into being,

"The Spirit of God was hovering over the surface of the waters." (Genesis 1:2)

The earth began to take shape and every living plant and creature was made as the Lord continued to speak "life". Eventually, creating humankind, in His own image, the Lord commanded them to be *fruitful.*

"So God created human beings in his own image. In the image of God he created them; male and female he created them. Then God blessed them and said, 'Be fruitful and multiply.'" (Genesis 1:27-28)

We can see that the desire we have for our lives to grow, to be fruitful and make a difference, comes from a God-ordained blessing and mandate that was spoken over us at creation.

There is a further truth we can take from the Genesis narrative that will help us grow in fruitfulness, I'm going to call the "after its own kind" principle.

"Then God said, 'Let the land sprout with vegetation – every sort of seed-bearing plant, and trees that grow seed-bearing fruit. These seeds will then produce the kinds of plants and trees from which they came.' And that is what happened. The land produced vegetation – all sorts of seed-bearing plants, and trees with seed-bearing fruit. Their seeds produced plants and trees of the same kind. And God saw that it was good." (Genesis 1: 11-12)

God made vegetation with seeds, giving it the capacity to multiply "after their own kind". It's why apples produce more apples and oaks produce more oaks.

The same was true of all the creatures that swam in the waters or flew in the sky.

"So God created great sea creatures and every living thing that scurries and swarms in the water, and every sort of bird – each producing offspring of the same kind. And God saw that it was good. Then God blessed them, saying, 'Be fruitful and multiply. Let the fish fill the seas, and let the birds multiply on the earth.'" (Genesis 1:22-22)

Also for animals:

"Then God said, 'Let the earth produce every sort of animal, each producing offspring of the same kind – livestock, small animals that scurry along the ground, and wild animals.' And that is what happened. God made all sorts of wild animals, livestock, and small animals, each able to produce offspring of the same kind. And God saw that it was good." (Genesis 1:24-25)

Fruitfulness "after its own kind" is a principle embedded in the created order. Similarly, as much as this principle is true for apples and oaks, it's true of the fruit produced in our lives.

Fruit produces after its own kind.

Jesus told His disciples that remaining in Him would cause their lives to be fruitful and bring great glory to His Father. We are going to explore how Jesus showed them that through Him their lives would produce fruit "after His (Jesus) own kind".

Paul helps us understand this further when he writes to the Galatians, explaining about the two very different kinds of fruit a person can produce: the sinful-nature-kind and the Holy-Spirit-(Jesus)-kind.

"When you follow the desires of your sinful nature, the results are very clear: sexual immorality, impurity, lustful pleasures, idolatry, sorcery, hostility, quarrelling, jealousy, outbursts of anger, selfish ambition, dissension, division, envy, drunkenness, wild parties, and other sins like these. Let me tell you again, as I have before, that anyone living that sort of life will not inherit the Kingdom of God. But the Holy Spirit produces this kind of fruit in our lives: love, joy, peace, patience, kindness, goodness, faithfulness, gentleness, and self-control. There is no law against these things! Those who belong to Christ Jesus have nailed the passions and desires of their sinful nature to his cross and crucified them there. Since we are living by the Spirit, let us follow the Spirit's leading in every part of our lives. Let us not become conceited, or provoke one another, or be jealous of one another." (Galatians 5: 19-26)

Over these next few days we are going to explore how we remain in Christ, rooted and able to bear fruit of the Jesus-kind.

Meditate on this:
"'I have loved you even as the Father has loved me. Remain in my love. When you obey my commandments, you remain in my love, just as I obey my Father's commandments and remain in his love. I have told you these things so that you will be filled with my joy. Yes, your joy will overflow!" (John 15: 9-11)

Going Deeper Still:

Think back over recent days and consider: the words you spoke, your attitudes and thoughts ... which fruits did you demonstrate from Paul's list to the Galatians?

Let's pray...

Jesus, I thank you that you love me. I thank you that you remain in the Father and I can remain in you. Today, will you help me by your Spirit to begin to see how I might remain in you even more? Amen.

DAY 2:
SPIRITUALLY SATURATED

———•———

"I have tried hard to find you – don't let me wander from your commands."
(Psalm 119:10)

Imagine a bowl filled nearly to the brim with water (not completely full, otherwise you will spill some). Next, imagine taking a sponge (the sort you might find in a bathroom) and plunging it into the water. As the water is absorbed, the sponge darkens; its dryness disappears and the water fills every pore. The sponge is now fully immersed in the water, completely saturated and, simultaneously the water is fully in the sponge. Is the water more in the sponge or the sponge more in the water? Of course, as long as the sponge remains immersed in the water, then the water will remain throughout the sponge.

Whilst the apostle John doesn't write about sponges, he does talk about something similar. He recounts an occasion when Jesus was with His disciples in the upper room, talking about what was to come, when He said,

"If you love me, obey my commandments. And I will ask the Father, and he will give you another Advocate, who will never leave you. He is the Holy Spirit, who leads into all truth. The world cannot receive him, because it isn't looking for him and doesn't recognize him. But you know him, because he lives with you now and later

will be in you. No, I will not abandon you as orphans – I will come
to you. Soon the world will no longer see me, but you will see me.
Since I live, you also will live. When I am raised to life again, you
will know that I am in my Father, and you are in me, and I am
in you. Those who accept my commandments and obey them are
the ones who love me. And because they love me, my Father will
love them. And I will love them and reveal myself to each of them."
(John 14:15-21)

I hope you're keeping up and know what sponge is in what
water! Our wholehearted love for Jesus means that we will choose
to obey Him and this confirms that we are *in Him*, even as He is
in the Father. And the Holy Spirit *in us*, even as we are *in Jesus*.

Remember how Jesus explained to His disciples why being in
Him was so vital?

*"Remain in me, and I will remain in you. For a branch cannot
produce fruit if it is severed from the vine, and you cannot be fruitful
unless you remain in me. Yes, I am the vine; you are the branches.
Those who remain in me, and I in them, will produce much fruit.
For apart from me you can do nothing."* (John 15:4-5)

What does it mean for us to remain in Christ – to be fully
immersed and filled, as if we are the sponge and Jesus is the water?
Are we fully immersed? Is there more of Jesus to seek, to find, to
know and to love?

The prophet Jeremiah wrote some encouraging words when he
prophesied what the Lord was saying:

*"'In those days when you pray, I will listen. If you look for me
wholeheartedly, you will find me. I will be found by you,' says the
Lord."* (Jeremiah 29:12-14a)

Jeremiah continued to foretell of the fruitfulness that was
coming to the people of God because of the Lord's love. This
fruitfulness would surpass all of the barren or difficult seasons

they had previously endured. From Scripture's timeless truth we can draw the same encouragement. God loved telling His people of the fruitfulness that was coming – and He says the same to us today.

"'This is what the Lord says: 'Those who survive the coming destruction will find blessings even in the barren land, for I will give rest to the people of Israel.' Long ago the Lord said to Israel: 'I have loved you, my people, with an everlasting love. With unfailing love I have drawn you to myself. I will rebuild you, my virgin Israel. You will again be happy and dance merrily with your tambourines. Again you will plant your vineyards on the mountains of Samaria and eat from your own gardens there. The day will come when watchmen will shout from the hill country of Ephraim, 'Come, let us go up to Jerusalem to worship the Lord our God.'"* (Jeremiah 31:2-6)

I'm a big fan of using Google Maps whenever I'm going on a long or unfamiliar car journey. I'm convinced I am a more courageous driver because of the little voice that chats to me from my mobile app! For my journey to be a success depends largely on two pieces of information: my starting point and my destination. Satellite systems are able to pick up the former and punching in the postcode of the latter enables the app to plan the route.

Seeking Jesus *wholeheartedly*, as Jeremiah said, makes Jesus our destination. Whatever starting point you find yourself at now, you can move forward towards Jesus, as the Holy Spirit enables.

Understanding your current position on your journey with Christ is so essential. Prayerfully considering how *full* or *immersed* you are in Christ will help identify your starting point.

Growing in Christ, filled with the Holy Spirit, means being able to move forward with confidence, knowing that you are getting nearer to where He wants you to be – even if you have to divert to get on the best road.

Mediate on this:

"Search me, O God, and know my heart; test me and know my anxious thoughts. Point out anything in me that offends you, and lead me along the path of everlasting life." (Psalm 139:23-24)

Going deeper still:

If you consider your life a bit like the image of the sponge (with Jesus as the water), then how immersed are you? Describe anything that might be holding you back. Ask the Holy Spirit to come and fill you afresh today.

Let's pray...

Lord, I thank you that you know me, every thought, every part of me. I thank you that you long for the whole of me to be in your presence, willingly, and filled with your Spirit wholeheartedly. Lord, I invite you to be in every part of me. Not just because you are everywhere, but because I long for you to be more in me and me in you. Amen.

DAY 3:
COMMIT COMPLETELY

—◦—

"Guide my steps by your word, so I will not be overcome by evil."
(Psalm 119:133)

My son came back from a rugby match, muddy and exhausted. Did I say he was muddy?! Looking past the aforementioned mud I asked him how the game had gone.

"Not good," came the disgruntled response.

His team had lost 8-3!

"Oh, what happened?" I asked carefully, aware that I was triggering a match-post-mortem. The conclusion was that it all came down to commitment. All of the boys were committed enough to show up, to put on their kit and get to the game. But, when it came to tackling the opposition, apparently there wasn't enough commitment. The commitment of being at the game needed to progress to being fully committed in the game.

I am reliably informed that at the point of committing your body to a tackle, your mind and muscle memory gang-up to remind you that *this is going to hurt!* But success in the game demands that even though it's going to hurt, the tackle must be made. Wholehearted commitment was the factor that would have taken the boys from looking like they were *at* the game to being fully *in* the game.

Paul wrote,

"Give yourselves completely to God, for you were dead, but now you have new life. So use your whole body as an instrument to do what is right for the glory of God. Sin is no longer your master, for you no longer live under the requirements of the law. Instead, you live under the freedom of God's grace." (Romans 6:13b-14)

Giving yourself completely to God means not holding anything back. You can't keep a part of yourself back, protecting it, keeping it in reserve. In choosing to trust Him wholeheartedly, and follow Him willingly, we have to commit completely. It won't hurt like committing to a rugby tackle, but it might sometimes feel bruising and there will be a cost.

Paul continues,

"...since God's grace has set us free from the law, does that mean we can go on sinning? Of course not! Don't you realize that you become the slave of whatever you choose to obey? You can be a slave to sin, which leads to death, or you can choose to obey God, which leads to righteous living. Thank God! Once you were slaves of sin, but now you wholeheartedly obey this teaching we have given you. Now you are free from your slavery to sin, and you have become slaves to righteous living." (Romans 6:15-18)

Remaining in Christ means wholeheartedly abandoning yourself to Him and giving up everything that would take you away from Him. It doesn't mean pursuing a list of rules and regulations, but it does mean being in pursuit of relationship.

To remain in Christ is to live as His disciple, wholeheartedly and completely committed to Him; living free from sin.

Before we get daunted about the challenge of being able to achieve this level of commitment, we need to remember the *who*, not the *what*! We shouldn't focus on *what* we can do to avoid sin, we should focus on the One *who* has done everything to enable us to be free from it. It's not about *what* we have to do to come into relationship with the Father, but about *who* has already done everything for us, so that we can.

In Exodus we read how God interrupted Moses with an attention grabbing, non-burning-up-burning-bush. God, wearing the bush as an outward sign of His presence, invited Moses to come closer. Then, much like a scene from *Mission Impossible*, He commissioned Moses to speak to Pharaoh to demand the release of the Israelites. The conclusion of the commission was that Moses would be the one to lead the released Israelites into freedom and the Promised Land! Obviously this was a big challenge to have been given, but Moses didn't grasp that however big the challenge was, God was even bigger. As a result, he struggled to commit.

"...'Who am I to appear before Pharaoh? Who am I to lead the people of Israel out of Egypt?' God answered, 'I will be with you. And this is your sign that I am the one who has sent you: When you have brought the people out of Egypt, you will worship God at this very mountain.' But Moses protested, 'If I go to the people of Israel and tell them, "The God of your ancestors has sent me to you," they will ask me, "What is his name?" Then what should I tell them?' God replied to Moses, 'I am who I am. Say this to the people of Israel: I am has sent me to you.' God also said to Moses, 'Say this to the people of Israel: Yahweh, the God of your ancestors – the God of Abraham, the God of Isaac, and the God of Jacob – has sent me to you. This is my eternal name, my name to remember for all generations.'" (Exodus 3: 11-15)

Moses felt too insignificant for his mission. While that may have been true, humanly speaking, he had missed something more important. In focusing on his weaknesses Moses missed the opportunity to focus on God's strengths. The supreme ability of God to succeed in this challenge did not register in Moses' mind. He looked at his *mission-impossible* and ignored his ultimate weapon – God Himself! Instead he focused on his own limitations.

I don't mean to give Moses a hard time, as I've known more than a few occasions when I've questioned, "Who am I?" But God was, is, and always will be bigger than any challenge we might face. Notice that whenever we have a challenge to confront, God Himself is always our answer. When Moses felt insignificant, God said, "I am." When Moses felt unable to communicate, God said, "I am." When Moses didn't feel brave enough, able enough, strong enough, intelligent enough, or suitable enough, God said, "But I am, I am, I am…"

Remaining in Him would have been enough for Moses. Remaining in Him would have brought about a harvest of freedom. He is always enough. God was, is, and always will be able! Moses said, "I'm not able", but God said, "I am."

Meditate on this:
"Therefore, since we are surrounded by such a huge crowd of witnesses to the life of faith, let us strip off every weight that slows us down, especially the sin that so easily trips us up. And let us run with endurance the race God has set before us. We do this by keeping our eyes on Jesus, the champion who initiates and perfects our faith. In the place of honour beside God's throne. Think of all the hostility he endured from sinful people; then you won't become weary and give up." (Hebrews 12:1-3)

Going deeper still:
As you consider how you are remaining in Christ, ask yourself where you are focusing the most – on the challenges you are facing or the Champion of your faith? What has God asked you to do that seems impossible? Which is bigger, the challenge or God?

Let's pray...

Thank you, Jesus, that you gave up everything for me. Please show me how I can commit wholeheartedly to you no matter what is ahead for me. Please help me understand that however great the challenges ahead of me, you are, and always will be, greater and more able. Amen.

DAY 4:
DELIGHT IN THE WHO

———•———

"I will delight in your decrees and not forget your word."
(Psalm 119:16)

When I was a child I was given an unusual plant called a Rose of Jericho. It looked a bit like a curled up, lifeless hedgehog! A brown ball of very dry twigs. Yet whenever this barren ball was placed on a saucer of water, roots down, it would come to life, opening up and expanding. Tiny woody petals uncurled from the inside. Sucking up life from the water, the rose turned from desert debris to oasis plant.

For years this plant occupied a little space in my bedroom. Occasionally I would dust it off to give it a drink and see it open up. It didn't require any significant care and seemed able to exist in its state of dry-dormancy.

But unlike a Rose of Jericho, we are not meant to live a life of mere survival and dryness, with only occasional refreshing. Instead, we are invited to be permanently rooted, drawing from the ultimate source of life.

The Psalmist wrote,

"Oh, the joys of those who do not follow the advice of the wicked, or stand around with sinners, or join in with mockers. But they delight in the law of the Lord, meditating on it day and night. They are like trees planted along the riverbank, bearing fruit each season.

Their leaves never wither, and they prosper in all they do." (Psalm 1:1-3)

This Psalmist tells us that meditating day and night on the law of the Lord is like being planted along a riverbank. He uses the analogy of a plant that is nourished and refreshed constantly – vastly different from what my poor, un-rooted Rose of Jericho experienced.

The Psalmist encourages an around-the-clock focus on God's Word – both "day and night". To be able to enjoy a fruitful life the believer must first delight in the Word of God. The Word is essential for us to grow as disciples.

I love the Word of God and will always seek to encourage people to go deeper into it. Through this book I'm cheering you on to go deeper in your love and appreciation for God's Word. However, real fruitfulness abounds when we understand not just *what* we are reading, but *who* we are encountering in the Word.

One of Jesus' closest disciples, John, explains this for us:

"In the beginning the Word already existed. The Word was with God, and the Word was God. He existed in the beginning with God. God created everything through him, and nothing was created except through him. The Word gave life to everything that was created, and his life brought light to everyone. The light shines in the darkness, and the darkness can never extinguish it." (John 1:1-5)

And,

"So the Word became human and made his home among us. He was full of unfailing love and faithfulness. And we have seen his glory, the glory of the Father's one and only Son." (John 1:14)

The Word became flesh, came to earth, and was called Jesus. When we draw closer to the Word of God we are drawing closer to Jesus. When we go deeper into the written Word, our roots will grow deeper into the Living Word. Knowing the Word of God is essential for us to be able to bear fruit.

Jesus said,

"Yes, I am the vine; you are the branches. Those who remain in me, and I in them, will produce much fruit. For apart from me you can do nothing." (John 15:5)

Jesus is the vine to which we are connected. His Word is the "riverbank" in which we are planted. It's not what we are planted in, but who that matters. It is being rooted in Him that will cause us to live a fruitful life. Being planted in Jesus enables love, rather than law, to transform us. As we grow in love for Him, it is that love that makes us want to fulfil the law, not the law that inspires us to love.

Paul referred to his own transformation story from legalism to freedom in his letter to the Philippians:

"...I was a member of the Pharisees, who demand the strictest obedience to the Jewish law. I was so zealous that I harshly persecuted the church. And as for righteousness, I obeyed the law without fault. I once thought these things were valuable, but now I consider them worthless because of what Christ has done. Yes, everything else is worthless when compared with the infinite value of knowing Christ Jesus my Lord. For his sake I have discarded everything else, counting it all as garbage, so that I could gain Christ and become one with him. I no longer count on my own righteousness through obeying the law; rather, I become righteous through faith in Christ. For God's way of making us right with himself depends on faith. I want to know Christ and experience the mighty power that raised him from the dead. I want to suffer with him, sharing in his death, so that one way or another I will experience the resurrection from the dead!" (Philippians 3: 5-11)

Paul came to the realisation that the law, without Christ, was no more than "garbage". A more accurate translation of Paul's description of a Christ-less faith is "dung". You get the picture – this is not a life to treasure, but rather one to discard. But, Paul knew that life in Christ had infinite value.

Meditate on this:

"From his abundance we have all received one gracious blessing after another. For the law was given through Moses, but God's unfailing love and faithfulness came through Jesus Christ. No one has ever seen God. But the unique One, who is himself God, is near to the Father's heart. He has revealed God to us." (John 1:16-18)

Going deeper still:

Consider what, or who, you are rooted into. What is the truth that you focus on the most?

Let's pray...

Lord, I thank you so much that in your Word I will always encounter you. Thank you that meeting you in your Word will lead to a fruitfulness in my life in every season. I choose to dig into your Word more than I have done before. Amen.

DAY 5:
THE POSTURE OF PERMISSION
———•———

"You made me; you created me. Now give me the sense to follow
your commands."
(Psalm 119:73)

Today we are going to stay with the message of Psalm 1 a little
longer. The Psalmist encouraged more than just simply being
rooted in the Word of God in order to become fruitful. He also
recognised a relational challenge, which is still pertinent for
us today. The challenge of choosing to be selective about who
influences the fruitful outcomes in our life.

"Oh, the joys of those who do not follow the advice of the wicked,
or stand around with sinners, or join in with mockers. But they
delight in the law of the Lord, meditating on it day and night."
(Psalm 1:1-2)

Throughout His public ministry Jesus was seen in the company
of a vast array of people. He was known to fraternise with people
from all walks of life – tax collectors, prostitutes, lepers, the
religious, the non-religious. Many of his companions were seen as
community misfits – most of whom were especially unfavourable
in the eyes of those trying to be religiously perfect with God's law:
the Pharisees.

One time as...

"...Jesus left the town, he saw a tax collector named Levi sitting

29

at his tax collector's booth. 'Follow me and be my disciple,' Jesus said to him. So Levi got up, left everything, and followed him. Levi held a banquet in his home with Jesus as the guest of honour. Many of Levi's fellow tax collectors and other guests also ate with them. But the Pharisees and their teachers of religious law complained bitterly to Jesus' disciples: 'Why do you eat and drink with such scum?' Jesus answered them, 'Healthy people don't need a doctor – sick people do. I have come to call not those who think they are righteous, but those who know they are sinners and need to repent.'" (Luke 5:27-32)

The Pharisees, concerned with religious compromise, were appalled at the choices Jesus made. Trying to be obedient to the letter of the law, they challenged Jesus at every opportunity. However, Jesus, a Rabbi, knew the Old Testament scriptures perfectly. He had studied them to such depth that He could recite them by heart. So how did Jesus reconcile the tension between the "undesirable" company He kept with the Psalmist's challenge?

The answer was all in His posture!

The Psalmist didn't warn against sitting with non-believers, hanging out with them and being friends with them. Rather he warned of *following* their advice, *standing* with them, and *joining in* with them. He was warning us not to be influenced by those heading in a different direction from the Lord. To follow the advice of someone is to become their follower.

Remember, the fruit we are seeking to produce in our lives comes from being rooted in Jesus. It is fruit *after His kind.*

Jesus kept company with all kinds of needy people in order that *they* could follow *Him*. Jesus neither allowed Himself to become anyone else's follower, nor compromised what He was there to do. Jesus didn't align Himself with the behaviour of others or get drawn into their activities. Far from it. He invited them to join in with Him.

Remember the time when Peter didn't like what Jesus said was going to happen and as a result tried to alter the outcome?

"From then on Jesus began to tell his disciples plainly that it was necessary for him to go to Jerusalem, and that he would suffer many terrible things at the hands of the elders, the leading priests, and the teachers of religious law. He would be killed, but on the third day he would be raised from the dead. But Peter took him aside and began to reprimand him for saying such things. 'Heaven forbid, Lord,' he said. 'This will never happen to you!' Jesus turned to Peter and said, 'Get away from me, Satan! You are a dangerous trap to me. You are seeing things merely from a human point of view, not from God's.'" (Matthew 16:21-23)

Jesus loved Peter, but He was not there to follow Peter. He would not take the posture of follower, nor give Peter permission to tell Him what He should be doing.

Our fruitfulness will be impacted by who we are following. Growing in our follower-ship of Christ will enable us to grow in fruitfulness. We must allow our perspective to be shaped by God's perspective. We must follow Christ rather than trying to get Him to follow us. This is not to say we won't ever take human advice and counsel, but we make a conscious decision not to take the wrong people's advice and counsel.

Following the wisdom and guidance of those who are not following God is to be led in a different direction. Paul wrote about followers of Jesus being together as a team, wanting to see the same results, sharing the same vision and purpose. He wrote to the believers in Corinth saying,

"Don't team up with those who are unbelievers. How can righteousness be a partner with wickedness? How can light live with darkness? What harmony can there be between Christ and

the devil? How can a believer be a partner with an unbeliever? And what union can there be between God's temple and idols? For we are the temple of the living God. As God said: 'I will live in them and walk among them. I will be their God, and they will be my people. Therefore, come out from among unbelievers, and separate yourselves from them, says the Lord. Don't touch their filthy things, and I will welcome you. And I will be your Father, and you will be my sons and daughters, says the Lord Almighty.'" (2 Corinthians 6:14 18)

As this journey continues we will further consider how our "posture of permission" determines who we allow to influence us and who we choose to follow. We can work with, study with, and be friends with many people from all kinds of backgrounds, but we don't have to assume a posture of permission and let them determine the course of our spiritual life.

Meditate on this:

"'If you don't personally go with us, don't make us leave this place. How will anyone know that you look favourably on me – on me and on your people – if you don't go with us? For your presence among us sets your people and me apart from all other people on the earth.' The Lord replied to Moses, 'I will indeed do what you have asked, for I look favourably on you, and I know you by name.'" (Exodus 33:15-17)

Going deeper:

Whose advice do you value the most and whose wisdom do you naturally seek out? Does this advice bring you closer to God or entice you further away from Him?

Let's pray...

Lord, I want to thank you for the people you have put in my life. Lord, will you increase my wisdom to choose the posture you desire – so that I don't give permission to the wrong people to determine the direction of my life? Amen.

DAY 6:
HABITS FOR HARVEST

———•———

*"Help me understand the meaning of your commandments, and I
will meditate on your wonderful deeds."*
(Psalm 119:27)

Consider for a moment some of your habits; the things you do
every day. Unless you are a naturist putting on clothes will be
a daily occurrence! Hopefully also washing, showering, teeth-
cleaning etc. Perhaps you have a favourite "must-have" drink first
thing in the morning, such as a coffee or tea (or in my case a green
tea with lemon, just in case you were wondering). Even those
working shift patterns, enduring topsy-turvy days, or night-owl
students, will have various habits peppered throughout each
twenty-four hours.

Why do we have these habits? Some habits are borne out of
well-practised routines that simply enable us to get done what
needs to be done. Getting to work or school on time rarely
happens by accident. Sometimes, our habits enable us to be
socially acceptable (that's the showering habit). Some habits are
good for us.

In Psalm 1 we're encouraged to develop a habit that is good
for us. A habit that comes with the promise of experiencing joy,
fruitfulness and prosperity. This habit is meditating on the law of
the Lord, day and night.

"Oh, the joys of those who do not follow the advice of the wicked, or stand around with sinners, or join in with mockers. But they delight in the law of the Lord, meditating on it day and night. They are like trees planted along the riverbank, bearing fruit each season. Their leaves never wither, and they prosper in all they do." (Psalm 1:1-3)

There are some religious practices which advocate meditation in order to empty our minds, in pursuit of a deeper sense of relaxation. However, biblical mediation is more about filling our mind. It is meditation designed to pause intentionally and reflect on truth; meditating to fill our mind with words of life and love. Biblical meditation is a habit that leads to fruitfulness, which is why I've included a verse or two to mediate on in each day of this devotional. The habit of repetition and focus will enable you to fill your mind and heart with life-changing truth.

As Paul wrote to Timothy,

"All Scripture is inspired by God and is useful to teach us what is true and to make us realise what is wrong in our lives. It corrects us when we are wrong and teaches us to do what is right. God uses it to prepare and equip his people to do every good work." (2 Timothy 3:16-17)

Delighting in the Word of God is good for us because we get to know what is right and wrong. Growing in the Word of God we become equipped for doing every good work. We will grow in knowing what is true. The Word of God is good for us. These are all good reasons why reading the Word of God is a great habit to grow. As Paul wrote to the Galatians,

"Don't be misled – you cannot mock the justice of God. You will always harvest what you plant. Those who live only to satisfy their own sinful nature will harvest decay and death from that sinful nature. But those who live to please the Spirit will harvest

everlasting life from the Spirit. So let's not get tired of doing what is good. At just the right time we will reap a harvest of blessing if we don't give up." (Galatians 6:7-9)

We are going to be establishing some good habits over these coming days. We are going deeper into the Word of God and planting seeds which will later bear a fruitful harvest in our lives.

I am currently in the early months of establishing a new habit – a gym habit! I was enticed with a too-good-to-refuse offer! Keenly aware that I'm too much of a fair-weather-runner, I decided to try a local gym. As a result my daily routine has had to change. And not just mine, my whole family's! To squeeze a gym session in before work I'm dropping my kids off to school earlier than before. They are almost still rubbing the sleep from their eyes when I'm opening the door to usher us all out. My kids are never going to be told off for being late to school as long as my gym-habit continues.

At the gym I'm making new friends who I would never otherwise have met; friendships where we encourage one another to persevere and show an interest in each other's days. These are real friendships in a new community.

So if a gym habit can benefit my kids' timekeeping at school, or the lives of friends in a community, how much more could my devotional habit impact my family and community?

My developing gym-habit routine is made that much easier by being a daily habit. Apparently, the more you do the less it hurts – or rather the quicker you recover! Furthermore, the more you do, the more you want to do! The same is true with meditating on the Word. The more we do, the more we want to do. The more we read, the more we see and understand. The more we get used to waking up half an hour earlier to read, the less it hurts! And remember that in the pages we are not just reading words, we are meeting with Jesus. So as our habit strengthens, so does our relationship with Jesus.

I have the privilege of being married to the most amazing man I know. Not only do we get to be family together, but we are best friends and co-workers. Tim is my absolute most favourite person on the planet. However, with all the opportunities I have to see Tim in my working day and in my family life, I still need to engage daily in our relationship. It is not enough to co-exist in life. To understand what he is thinking and feeling I need to engage in conversation – to listen and share myself wholeheartedly with him.

When Tim and I are apart we still connect by speaking on the phone or sending each other messages. We talk about our comings and goings, letting each other know where we are heading to and when we will be back together. We think about each other, pray for each other and consider each other even when apart. Whether we are in the same place or not, in the same town or country or not, we make every effort to stay connected, sharing in each other's experiences as much as we're able. It might not sound romantic, but we both make an effort to first *devote*, expecting to later delight in the *devotion*!

If it is not enough for me to spend a mere five minutes of rushed-time together with my life partner, how could it ever be enough for my relationship with Jesus?

To develop our relationship with Jesus we will benefit from developing some daily habits. What you are doing right now, in these moments, will impact your fruitfulness. Keep going – it is good for you!

Meditate on this:

"Trust in the Lord and do good. Then you will live safely in the land and prosper. Take delight in the Lord, and he will give you your heart's desires." (Psalm 37:3-4)

Going deeper still:

What would it look like for you to delight in the Lord even more than you do now? In what way can you fill your mind even more with Jesus? What can change in your daily routine to develop an even stronger devotional relationship and habit?

Let's pray...

Lord, please will you help me to do good and to strengthen good habits? Help me be open to being in your Word every day. Lord, I long for a harvest of fruitfulness in my life, so please help me establish good habits, like sowing seeds for harvest, that I might meet with you more closely and know you more intimately. May I delight in your Word, so that I might delight in you even more. Amen.

DAY 7:
DISTINCTLY DISTINCT

————•————

"I hate those with divided loyalties, but I love your instructions."
(Psalm 119:113)

As we continue to remain in Christ we will grow in demonstrating Kingdom fruitfulness. We will bear fruit that the world will recognise to be after Jesus' "own kind".

A couple of days ago we considered the "posture of permission" that we need to adopt as we consider who we are following. Our fruitfulness is influenced significantly by who we are following; who we spend our lives with. Herein lies a challenge for us as we remain in Christ, whilst continuing to live in the world: in what ways are our lives producing the distinctive fruit of the Kingdom of God, and not of the world?

Many years ago I had a conversation with a young woman – one which I've heard repeated by others all too often. She told me how thrilled she was that her non-Christian friends would say, "You're no different from us – even though you're a Christian." It made my heart sink that there was nothing that made her "different". Of course, it's wonderful to be able to connect with our friends and be relatable. But, if we're no different from our non-Christian friends, that is deeply troubling. We're meant to be different! Not higher, not better, not in a position to judge them, but different. Distinct. Witnesses of the One we love the most.

Jesus didn't want to "beam up" His disciples and rescue them from the perils of life on earth. Instead He gave them truth and set them free to show the world a different way – The Way.

He prayed to His Father,

"I have given them your word. And the world hates them because they do not belong to the world, just as I do not belong to the world. I'm not asking you to take them out of the world, but to keep them safe from the evil one. They do not belong to this world any more than I do. Make them holy by your truth; teach them your word, which is truth. Just as you sent me into the world, I am sending them into the world. And I give myself as a holy sacrifice for them so they can be made holy by your truth." (John 17:14-19)

We are not called from the world but sent to it. Why? Because Jesus loved the world so much that He came to save it. He came (and wants to keep coming to the world through us) so that more will be saved. How is this possible through us? It's all about the condition of the soil in which we are planted.

Jesus challenged His disciples saying,

"You are the salt of the earth. But what good is salt if it has lost its flavour? Can you make it salty again? It will be thrown out and trampled underfoot as worthless. You are the light of the world— like a city on a hilltop that cannot be hidden. No one lights a lamp and then puts it under a basket. Instead, a lamp is placed on a stand, where it gives light to everyone in the house. In the same way, let your good deeds shine out for all to see, so that everyone will praise your heavenly Father." (Matthew 5:13-16)

To understand this we need to understand the context in which Jesus spoke. In those days, salt wasn't just added to food to make it flavoursome – it was also used as a preservative, for its medicinal properties, and as a fertiliser!

In the absence of refrigeration technology, keeping food fresh was a big challenge. Meat was preserved by rubbing it with salt to extend its shelf life. Salt was used for its medicinal properties, with salty water being used to clean infected areas, hastening healing. Salt was also used as an active ingredient to increase the effectiveness of manure as a fertiliser, to enhance harvest! Salt was, of course, also used as an ingredient to bring out the best flavour in food. It's job wasn't to be the defining, overpowering taste, but rather to enhance the flavour of whatever food it was added to.

Familiar with the uses of salt in their communities, the disciples were challenged to be like salt themselves. Just like the first disciples, we too should preserve that which is good, heal those who are sick, and bring the best out of those around us. We need to mix into society in such a way that increased fruitfulness is the result. We are meant to be distinct to the world – otherwise we can't offer any difference, any preservation, any enhancement or any help.

Many years ago I worked in a hotel. I loved my job and was good at it. But for a long time afterwards I carried a regret from those days, until God kindly spoke to me about it. I just wasn't consistent in being *distinct* from my colleagues.

I was overly free in what I drank and not vigilant enough about the drinks bought for me by others. I blended in and offered little, or no, distinctive at all. As we've already recognised, Jesus was one to go to parties. He would hang out with all sorts of people, and often in circumstances that others considered distasteful – especially the religious authorities, who were constantly outraged. But, despite the company He kept, Jesus remained distinct. He offered an alternative: hope; a better way. He was in the world, but not like the world. The fruit that was produced from His life was not for His own pleasure – it fed, enhanced, preserved and healed others, causing them to become fruitful.

We can be so busy trying to "fit in" that we forget we are meant to "stand out". We can be so busy trying to blend in that we become bland and lose our saltiness. Remaining in Christ will lead to us living a life that stands out – one which enhances the world around us, preserves what's good and brings healing.

Meditate on this:

"I am praying not only for these disciples but also for all who will ever believe in me through their message. I pray that they will all be one, just as you and I are one – as you are in me, Father, and I am in you. And may they be in us so that the world will believe you sent me. I have given them the glory you gave me, so they may be one as we are one. I am in them and you are in me. May they experience such perfect unity that the world will know that you sent me and that you love them as much as you love me." (John 17:20-23)

Going Deeper Still:

In what ways have you blended with the world's ways? How can you become more rooted in truth in order to become more distinct, more like Jesus? How can you overcome the pressure to "fit in", and instead be able to "stand out" for Jesus even more?

Let's pray...

Lord, may I know what it is to be closer to you, more like you and less like the world so that you can, through me, show the world how much you love everyone. Amen.

DAY 8:
NEVER NEGLECT

———•———

*"Let me be united with all who fear you, with those who know
your laws."*
(Psalm 119:79)

Today we are going to continue on our journey towards fruitfulness
and turn our attention not only to who we are planted *in* but, who
we are planted *with*.

Years ago Tim and I visited the Sequoia National Park in
California – home to one of the largest trees on the planet. Sequoias
can grow beyond ninety four metres (three hundred feet) tall.
That is really tall whether in "old" or "new" measurements! Whilst
the Sequoia's average diameter is six to eight metres the largest
reported was a staggering seventeen metres wide. Some Sequoias
grow so big you can actually drive a car through tunnelled-out
archways. If that's not enough to impress, then the Giant Sequoia's
cone-capacity surely is. Some trees have up to eleven thousand
cones at any one time housing their bountiful supply of winged-
seeds!

However, it's not just their visible size and fruitfulness that's
impressive – it's also their roots. Unlike many trees Sequoias don't
anchor themselves with a strong tap root and so could actually
be toppled. Isolation is dangerous. Yet, they don't topple – simply
because they don't stand alone. Sequoias have a strong root system

which consists of countless outward growing roots that entwine with the roots of nearby sequoias forming mutually supportive security. They grow strong because they grow together.

The writer of Hebrews understood the principle of togetherness saying,

"Let us hold tightly without wavering to the hope we affirm, for God can be trusted to keep His promise. Let us think of ways to motivate one another to acts of love and good works. And let us not neglect our meeting together, as some people do, but encourage one another, especially now that the day of His return is drawing near." (Hebrews 10:23-25)

Still today we are encouraged by this text to seek ways to champion one another to good works and fruitfulness. To press on and persevere. To not waver from the hope we affirm, but to encourage one another to remain in Christ – together.

A challenge to us remaining in Christ is that sometimes we want to stay with Him but (let's be honest) we don't want to remain in the church. Even as a church leader I've known this feeling! However, the Church is God's body represented here on earth. We might not be body-perfect, but the body is essential to life. Separating from church would be like us being an arm and cutting ourselves off from the body. Doing this we can't be surprised when the arm loses its pulse and becomes useless. Furthermore, the body is also damaged and suffers a life-threatening haemorrhage. Not to mention the challenge of life without the use of an arm! It's not good for the arm or the body. Similarly, it's not good for us personally or collectively to be separated. We need to stay connected.

As Paul says, *"All of you together are Christ's body, and each of you is a part of it."* (1 Corinthians 12:27)

We can read this and miss the big-picture and tiny-detail

of the Church. There are 2.18 billion followers of Christ in the world, and yet each member of the Church has a name; most are part of a local church. In his day Paul wrote mostly to small house churches – believers meeting in small shops and corners of courtyards. He wrote to the people of Corinth, Ephesus, and Rome, amongst others. Yet his urge for us to stay connected and to never neglect the church still resonates to us today.

Fruitful Christ-followers discover their place in the body of Christ. Perhaps our little church is merely a limb on Christ's body for the town we love. And perhaps I'm just a fingernail, but I know that I only make sense as part of the body. The way that God designed them, even fingernails have a purpose and bring strength to our grip, as well as control to the finest stroke of a pen. When it comes to the wider Church we all recognise that there are denominations, particular streams of expression, carrying unique gifting and anointing across a broad spectrum. Greater strength and fruitfulness comes with uniting across the divides of denomination. Paul warned the Corinthians, who were being tempted to divide according to the specific leader of their stream, saying, *"...Each of us did the work the Lord gave us. I planted the seed in your hearts, and Apollos watered it, but it was God who made it grow. It's not important who does the planting, or who does the watering. What's important is that God makes the seed grow."* (1 Corinthians 3:5-7)

With so much difference and potential for division it is not surprising that Paul was strong in urging the believers to, *"Always be humble and gentle. Be patient with each other, making allowance for each other's faults because of your love. Make every effort to keep yourselves united in the Spirit, binding yourselves together with peace. For there is one body and one Spirit, just as you have been called to one glorious hope for the future. There is one Lord,*

45

one faith, one baptism, one God and Father of all, who is over all, in all, and living through all." (Ephesians 4:2-6)

What is it to make every effort to keep united in the Spirit? Effort can be defined as a "vigorous or determined attempt". Peter, writing his first letter to the believers, urged them all to bring their gifts and be strong body-parts saying, *"God has given each of you a gift from his great variety of spiritual gifts. Use them well to serve one another. Do you have the gift of speaking? Then speak as though God himself were speaking through you. Do you have the gift of helping others? Do it with all the strength and energy that God supplies. Then everything you do will bring glory to God through Jesus Christ."* (1 Peter 4:10-11)

We need to hold on to each other as we hold onto Christ whilst also giving ourselves wholeheartedly. Our wholehearted commitment to Jesus (which we explored on day three) will lead to a wholehearted commitment to the Body of Christ – His Church – our local church (and beyond our borders). Who are we rooted with and how well are we connected?

Our relationships with others matter – across our own congregations, across year groups in our school Christian unions, colleges and universities, across the churches in our villages, towns and cities, amongst the churches in our denominations and networks. We can grow stronger and more fruitful when we grow together; this brings the Father glory.

Are we making every effort? We must bear with one another in love and choose to focus more on what unites us than what divides. Let the Holy Spirit fill the spaces between us. Our every effort will involve prayer, humility, conversations, forgiveness, repentance, more humility, grace, and above all love. All of the fruit that comes from remaining in Christ will be needed to keep us united and remaining with His body. Never neglect the connections.

Meditate on this:

"Don't think you are better than you really are. Be honest in your evaluation of yourselves, measuring yourselves by the faith God has given us. Just as our bodies have many parts and each part has a special function, so it is with Christ's body. We are many parts of one body, and we all belong to each other. In his grace, God has given us different gifts for doing certain things well." (Romans 12: 3b-6a)

Going deeper still:

Where has Christ positioned you in His Body? How can you connect more deeply in your church? How can you grow in being an encouragement to others that you, and they, might grow stronger and more fruitful?

Let's pray...

Lord, forgive me for the times when I have neglected important relationships in your church. Help me to grow in my belonging to the family that you have connected me with – or help me find a church family to connect with – so that I might grow more rooted and then become more fruitful. Amen.

DAY 9:
PARTNERING FOR FRUITFULNESS

"I told you my plans, and you answered. Now teach me your decrees."
(Psalm 119: 26)

Some time ago our denomination engaged with some missions work in Southern Sudan. For a number of years my husband, and small team from AoG, repeatedly visited a remote Sudanese village called Adoor. They stayed in the heart of the community in primitive "tukul" huts, some twenty four hours drive in any direction from the nearest tarmac road. The villagers were desperately poor, blighted by tribal wars, desperate for help.

One key focus of our missions work has always been to partner in such a way that we don't become the essential ingredient to the survival of the villagers. We don't want to create an unhealthy dependence. Rather, we set out to support, equip and resource others, helping them not merely to survive, but even thrive without us. The building of wells, the establishing of schools, micro-financing businesses, and the planting of churches is all undertaken with this aim in mind.

One year Tim arranged for an agricultural scientist to join the small mission team to analyse the soil in and around the Sudanese village – the aim being that we could then help them understand what crops might actually be able to grow. This would enable them to grow essential food for themselves and also additional crops which they could trade with neighbouring villages.

Discovering that the soil was fertile, we provided them with a supply of seeds and made sure they knew exactly what to do. The next year Tim went back expecting to see the harvest. There was nothing! Even though there had been favourable weather, there were no crops. No fruitfulness, no signs of new life, no stall at the market. Over the next few days the realisation dawned that whilst they said they wanted things to change, these precious people didn't actually want to be part of the solution. They were happy to receive support, but they didn't want to work the land. The ploughs and the oxen were sold off, and the seeds were never planted or nurtured. There was nothing to harvest. The soil was fertile, but it gave no yield because people wouldn't yield their efforts to sow the seeds.

As Paul said to the Galatians, *"Don't be misled – you cannot mock the justice of God. You will always harvest what you plant."* (Galatians 6:7)

Paul wrote to the Colossians wanting to see those precious people thrive in a life of faithful follower-ship of Christ; to live fruitful lives, so that Christ's glory would be revealed and His Kingdom extended.

Aware that the people of Colossae could not do this alone, Paul wrote to them to teach and encourage them to persevere in their faith.

"So we have not stopped praying for you since we first heard about you. We ask God to give you complete knowledge of his will and to give you spiritual wisdom and understanding. Then the way you live will always honour and please the Lord, and your lives will produce every kind of good fruit. All the while, you will grow as you learn to know God better and better." (Colossians 1:9-10)

However much Paul prayed and the Lord provided the spiritual wisdom, there was still the need for the people to co-operate and partner with the Holy Spirit – living in such a way that they would honour and please the Lord. Only then the abundant harvest of every kind of good fruit would come.

Now here is where we need to understand something about this little word called "wisdom" which, along with understanding, will lead to "every kind of good fruit". It doesn't come easy! This is what broke our hearts for our Sudanese friends. Their challenges were not going to be solved with a quick fix, but rather a different way of living. James gives us some clear insight when he wrote,

"Dear brothers and sisters, when troubles of any kind come your way, consider it an opportunity for great joy. For you know that when your faith is tested, your endurance has a chance to grow. So let it grow, for when your endurance is fully developed, you will be perfect and complete, needing nothing. If you need wisdom, ask our generous God, and he will give it to you. He will not rebuke you for asking. But when you ask him, be sure that your faith is in God alone. Do not waver, for a person with divided loyalty is as unsettled as a wave of the sea that is blown and tossed by the wind. Such people should not expect to receive anything from the Lord. Their loyalty is divided between God and the world, and they are unstable in everything they do." (James 1:2-8)

When it came to understanding about spiritual wisdom Paul and James both knew the same thing – wisdom rarely came simply by heavenly download. Rather wisdom came through persevering in the face of adversity. It is accompanied by joy because of the certainty of what is being gained through what is being endured.

It is not so much what you endure but rather how you endure it. This is what Paul meant when he said, *"then the way you live will always honour and please the Lord, and your lives will produce every kind of good fruit. All the while, you will grow as you learn to know God better and better."* (Colossians 1:10)

As James said, walking with unwavering loyalty to God will produce a confidence and stability in all circumstances. Conversely, having divided loyalties, being double-minded, will cause instability during life's storms and will restrict our ability to receive anything from God.

Our fruitfulness, from remaining in Christ, is an active partnership. It's not a passive, one-sided deal. Our Sudanese friends wanted something from us, but didn't want to do anything with us – even if it was for their good.

Fruitful discipleship is about engaging in a partnership with God, sowing the seeds He gives us and working the land He has entrusted to us, bearing fruit in His way, for His glory.

Meditate on this:

"I no longer call you slaves, because a master doesn't confide in his slaves. Now you are my friends, since I have told you everything the Father told me. You didn't choose me. I chose you. I appointed you to go and produce lasting fruit, so that the Father will give you whatever you ask for, using my name. This is my command: Love each other." (John 15: 15-17)

Going deeper still:

What do you want the Lord to do for you? In what ways might He want you to be part of the answer, to work in partnership and friendship with you?

Let's pray...

Lord, thank you that you don't want me to be isolated but to be connected, partnering with your Spirit to see my life become fruitful, for the Father's glory. Help me today to co-operate with you. Amen.

DAY 10:
WAITING WITH HOPE

———•———

"Lord, you are mine! I promise to obey your words!"
(Psalm 119:57)

Isaiah said, *"Have you not known? Have you not heard? The everlasting God, the Lord, the Creator of the ends of the earth, neither faints nor is weary. His understanding is unsearchable. He gives power to the weak, and to those who have no might He increases strength. Even the youths shall faint and be weary, and the young men shall utterly fall, but those who wait on the Lord shall renew their strength; they shall mount up with wings like eagles, they shall run and not be weary, they shall walk and not faint."* (Isaiah 40:28-31 NKJV)

As I woke up, the general anaesthetic wearing off, I found myself crying. To be honest, I'm not sure why I was crying – but there I was, staring at the hospital ceiling. Crying. I was getting married in a few months and yet, in that moment, I was recovering from a procedure that was an attempt to explore why I was having gynaecological challenges. My future fertility was under the microscope. Results would not be instant, so I went home and the wait began. Diagnosis was going to lead to a poor fertility prognosis. However, I had a choice to make: would I wait with, or without, hope? My response would be influenced by either what I was waiting for, or who I was waiting with.

Paul understood waiting!

"If we already have something, we don't need to hope for it. But if we look forward to something we don't yet have, we must wait patiently and confidently." (Romans 8:24-25)

Remember how Paul challenged the believers in Colossae about living their lives in such a way that they pleased God? It is in the living – and in the waiting – that there is relational revelation. *"... All the while, you will grow as you learn to know God better and better"* (Colossians 1:10).

The prophet Habakkuk was deeply concerned about the prosperity of the unrighteous and the atrocities he saw around him. Desperate for the Lord to move and bring about a wave of righteous restoration, he implored the Lord to show where justice would prevail.

Now, the story of Habakkuk might not seem to be totally encouraging, because the Lord tells him that things are going to get worse before they get any better. But even in the promise of more trouble there is a truth we can take hold of. When the Lord promises something it will come to pass. When we wait on the Lord we can do so with hope. Furthermore, as the Lord's purposes are revealed to us, we can grow in our awareness of His presence. We read that,

"This vision is for a future time. It describes the end, and it will be fulfilled. If it seems slow in coming, wait patiently, for it will surely take place. It will not be delayed." (Habakkuk 2:3)

However, the tide would one day turn:

"For as the waters fill the sea, the earth will be filled with an awareness of the glory of the Lord." (Habakkuk 2:14)

As we have already seen, remaining in Christ is not about *what* we will get out of our wait, but *who* we will get out of it. It is not about *what* we are waiting for, but *who* we are waiting with.

It is not about *what* trial we are experiencing, but *who* we are experiencing the trial with.

Habakkuk's beautiful reply reveals his unwavering, undivided loyalty as he responds to this devastation saying,

"I trembled inside when I heard this; my lips quivered with fear. My legs gave way beneath me, and I shook in terror. I will wait quietly for the coming day when disaster will strike the people who invade us. Even though the fig trees have no blossoms, and there are no grapes on the vines; even though the olive crop fails, and the fields lie empty and barren; even though the flocks die in the fields, and the cattle barns are empty, yet I will rejoice in the Lord! I will be joyful in the God of my salvation! The Sovereign Lord is my strength! He makes me as surefooted as a deer, able to tread upon the heights." (Habakkuk 3:16-19)

Habakkuk went from knee-knocking fear to standing as surefooted as a deer. He knew that in the tests of his life, remaining in and waiting with God would enable him to go from being weak to strong. He moved from scrabbling in grassy fields to confidently traversing mountains and hills. Jumping, leaping, sure-footed. Knowing who he walked with enabled him to be confident about what he walked on. Habakkuk's loyalty to the Lord was not dependent on seeing fruitfulness, but rather his fruitfulness was dependent on his loyalty. Habakkuk would worship through the tears, in spite of the fears. He worshipped throughout every year – even in trial and difficulty, barrenness, disaster and need. Habakkuk would remain undivided in his loyalty and allow the Lord to be his strength and his hope. There might not have been a fruitfulness surrounding Habakkuk but there was a fruitfulness within him. He had hope.

Paul expressed this so well to the believers in Rome when he said,

"Because of our faith, Christ has brought us into this place of undeserved privilege where we now stand, and we confidently and joyfully look forward to sharing God's glory. We can rejoice, too, when we run into problems and trials, for we know that they help us develop endurance. And endurance develops strength of character, and character strengthens our confident hope of salvation. And this hope will not lead to disappointment. For we know how dearly God loves us, because He has given us the Holy Spirit to fill our hearts with his love. When we were utterly helpless, Christ came at just the right time and died for us sinners. Now, most people would not be willing to die for an upright person, though someone might perhaps be willing to die for a person who is especially good. But God showed His great love for us by sending Christ to die for us while we were still sinners. And since we have been made right in God's sight by the blood of Christ, He will certainly save us from God's condemnation. For since our friendship with God was restored by the death of his Son while we were still his enemies, we will certainly be saved through the life of His Son. So now we can rejoice in our wonderful new relationship with God because our Lord Jesus Christ has made us friends of God." (Romans 5:2-11)

Remaining in Christ enables us to live our life in such a way that it will honour and bless Him. We can grow in wisdom and understanding, enabling us to get to know the Lord better. All of this is possible because Jesus chose not to remain in Heaven, but rather gave up His life, so that He could be in our lives. This is the beautiful grace and glory of the Gospel. Hope only comes through remaining in Christ. Even if we have to wait, we can wait with hope.

Meditate on this:

"But blessed are those who trust in the Lord and have made the Lord their hope and confidence." (Jeremiah 17:7)

Going deeper still:

Consider what you are waiting for. In what ways might you grow in hope as you are waiting in the Lord (rather than growing the desire of what you want from the Lord)? In what ways have you already experienced Him renewing you, lifting you, strengthening and encouraging you – even as you've waited?

Let's pray...

Thank you, Jesus that as I remain in you – however wobbly my knees feel – you can make me confident and courageous as my hope in you is assured. Please help me know and live this in my day today. Amen.

DAY 11:
HIDDEN TREASURES

———•———

"I will pursue your commands, for you expand my understanding."
(Psalm 119:32)

On holiday last year our family took a day-trip to explore the caves in Britain's beautiful Cheddar Gorge. We joined the tourists, plugged ourselves into an audio-tour and proceeded to gawp our way through the rocky caverns hidden beneath the earth's surface. We were stunned by its majestic beauty.

Here's a quick history lesson if you are unfamiliar: Richard Gough discovered the Cheddar Gorge caves in the 1800s. After months, even years of research and exploration, he discovered a spectacle displaying a myriad of colours, textures and shapes. Underground mountains and valleys carved out by the hand of God using water and time.

As our audio tour continued, one story particularly grabbed my attention. One night Richard had squeezed his way through to a previously undiscovered cave. Standing up and shining his lamp, his breath was taken away as his eyes were captivated by something no one else had ever seen. Rather surprisingly, he didn't stay there for a long time, soaking in the scene or documenting the discovery. Instead, he rapidly reversed out of the cave and rushed home. Excitedly, he woke his family and led them all back, retracing his steps to see the new cave for themselves. This discovery had been too incredible to keep to himself. So there they all stood, amazed. Richard called the cave Solomon's Temple. There, the explorer, his wife, and sons spent the remainder of the night singing hymns and praising God.

Even in the darkest, most "underground" of places it is possible to see the signs, follow the clues and discover the presence of God. When we do, the only natural response is to share the good news, and to worship.

As the prophet Isaiah wrote:

"I will give you treasures hidden in the darkness— secret riches. I will do this so you may know that I am the Lord, the God of Israel, the one who calls you by name." (Isaiah 45:3)

Growing our roots into the Word of God is like discovering hidden treasures underground; secret riches in which we discover the Lord Himself – the one who is calling us, by our name, to come. Inviting us to put our roots down and go deeper and deeper to discover hidden treasures.

Jesus told a parable about discovering treasure:

"The Kingdom of Heaven is like a treasure that a man discovered hidden in a field. In his excitement, he hid it again and sold everything he owned to get enough money to buy the field. Again, the Kingdom of Heaven is like a merchant on the lookout for choice pearls. When he discovered a pearl of great value, he sold everything he owned and bought it!" (Matthew 13:44-46)

The invitation today is to value what we discover as we go deep in the Word of God, and as Christ Himself is revealed to us. Will we value this deepening revelation of treasure more than anything else? Will we recognise the beauty of what He wants us to see? This treasure must not stay hidden.

One of our holiday discoveries in the Cheddar Gorge was the consistency of the caves' core temperature. No matter how scorching the sunshine is above ground (in the UK, I can but dream!), or conversely how cold it is, the temperature in the caves never changes. It remains at a steady eleven degrees – the perfect temperature for maturing cheddar!

Similarly, our rootedness in the depth of the Living Word will bring a consistency to our lives. Whether we find ourselves in the "heat" of pressure or the "cold" of isolation; no matter what is going on around us, when Christ is at the core of us, we can still be fruitful.

The prophet Jeremiah wrote:

"Cursed are those who put their trust in mere humans, who rely on human strength and turn their hearts away from the Lord. They are like stunted shrubs in the desert, with no hope for the future. They will live in the barren wilderness, in an uninhabited salty land. But blessed are those who trust in the Lord and have made the Lord their hope and confidence. They are like trees planted along a riverbank, with roots that reach deep into the water. Such trees are not bothered by the heat or worried by long months of drought. Their leaves stay green, and they never stop producing fruit." (Jeremiah 17:5-8)

Whatever is going on around us; however terrifying or worrying it is, we can remain rooted in the Word enabling us to live with confidence in Christ. Whatever challenges we face – whether they are to do with health, relationships, bereavement, employment, community, national or local conflict – we can remain rooted and confident in the Lord Himself. Not bothered by heat or drought, our rootedness in His Word produces true and consistent faith in us.

In 1871 a man called Horatio Spafford tragically lost his two year old son to Scarlet Fever. Further catastrophe quickly struck when he lost all of his wealth in the Great Chicago Fire. Deciding to escape the adversity, he planned for his family to holiday in Europe. Delayed personally by business, Horatio's wife, Anna, and their four remaining children travelled ahead to Europe by boat. On the journey, the boat carrying the family struck another vessel causing their boat to sink. All four of the children were drowned, only Spafford's wife, Anna, survived. Heartbroken with grief, Spafford set sail to join his wife. Passing the point on the water where his children had drowned, he was inspired to pen a song. You might have heard of it: *It is Well with My Soul.*

When peace, like a river, attendeth my way,
When sorrows like sea billows roll;
Whatever my lot, Thou hast taught me to say,
It is well, it is well with my soul.

It is well with my soul,
It is well, it is well with my soul.

Though Satan should buffet, though trials should come,
Let this blest assurance control,
That Christ hath regarded my helpless estate,
And hath shed His own blood for my soul.

My sin – oh, the bliss of this glorious thought! –
My sin, not in part but the whole,
Is nailed to the cross, and I bear it no more,
Praise the Lord, praise the Lord, O my soul!

For me, be it Christ, be it Christ hence to live:
If Jordan above me shall roll,
No pang shall be mine, for in death as in life
Thou wilt whisper Thy peace to my soul.

But, Lord, 'tis for Thee, for Thy coming we wait,
The sky, not the grave, is our goal;
Oh, trump of the angel! Oh, voice of the Lord!
Blessed hope, blessed rest of my soul!

And Lord, haste the day when the faith shall be sight,
The clouds be rolled back as a scroll;
The trump shall resound, and the Lord shall descend,
Even so, it is well with my soul.

Meditate on this:

"My child, listen to what I say, and treasure my commands. Tune your ears to wisdom, and concentrate on understanding. Cry out for insight, and ask for understanding. Search for them as you would for silver; seek them like hidden treasures. Then you will understand what it means to fear the Lord, and you will gain knowledge of God. For the Lord grants wisdom! From his mouth come knowledge and understanding." (Proverbs 2:1-6)

Going deeper still:

What previously hidden truths from Scripture do you hold to, so that no matter what goes on around, you can be like Jeremiah and Horatio, and say that all is well with your soul?

Let's pray...

Father, I thank you for your presence in my life; that because of your presence I can say that it is well with my soul. May this song be in my heart and on my lips today. Amen.

DAY 12:
SEEDS AND SOILS

---·---

"Lord, sustain me as you promised, that I may live! Do not let my
hope be crushed."
(Psalm 119:116)

In one of Jesus' most well-known parables He tells the story of a
farmer scattering seeds. Many seeds were thrown and they landed
in one of four ways, meaning that, as a result, one in four was
harvested. Firstly, some seeds fell on the footpath to be consumed
by opportunist birds. Secondly, some seeds fell on rocky soil.
There was enough soil for a quick response, but these shallow-
rooted plants produced a flimsy crop which simply died away.
Thirdly, some seeds fell amongst thorns where they grew up, but
were choked by the thorns and so perished. Finally, some seeds
fell on fertile soil where their roots went down and they sprouted
successfully. With deep, strong roots plunging into good soil
these plants were not easily consumed by predators, overpowered
or stifled. These seeds were said to produce a harvest that was,
"...thirty, sixty, and even a hundred times as much as had been
planted" (Mark 4:8).

Unlike most of His parables, which Jesus allowed to go
unexplained, on this occasion He took the opportunity to make
sure the interpretation was clear:

"The farmer plants seed by taking God's word to others. The seed

that fell on the footpath represents those who hear the message, only to have Satan come at once and take it away. The seed on the rocky soil represents those who hear the message and immediately receive it with joy. But since they don't have deep roots, they don't last long. They fall away as soon as they have problems or are persecuted for believing God's word. The seed that fell among the thorns represents others who hear God's word, but all too quickly the message is crowded out by the worries of this life, the lure of wealth, and the desire for other things, so no fruit is produced. And the seed that fell on good soil represents those who hear and accept God's word and produce a harvest of thirty, sixty, or even a hundred times as much as had been planted!" (Mark 4:14-20)

Sometimes I've wondered if these different types of soil represent four different types of person, or one person in four different seasons of life. Could all of them be me – or you?

Consider the "footpath person" – the one who hears the message, but has it immediately snatched away by the enemy. This is an all-too-familiar strategy of the enemy, first revealed in the Creation narrative. Adam and Eve were blessed with a carefree, shame-free life with each other and God. But the enemy's snatch strategy was soon revealed as he came to cast doubt on what Eve knew. He questioned her, *"Did God really say you must not eat the fruit from any of the trees in the garden?"* (Genesis 3:1). We know from the text that God had previously said, *"You may freely eat the fruit of every tree in the garden – except the tree of the knowledge of good and evil. If you eat its fruit, you are sure to die"* (Genesis 2:16b-17). However, the enemy was able to cast doubt in Eve's mind and the snatch began.

If truth is not well rooted in Christ then it can be snatched away and consumed by doubt. However, there is a way of preventing this – of holding on tight to truth. Jesus tells us how this can be done and we will come back to this shortly.

Before that, what about the "rocky soil person"? Those that Jesus said would hear and recognise truth, accepting it quickly. Tragically, it was a surface-level acceptance that meant life's troubles would quickly overwhelm them and the truth would simply disappear.

Rocky-soil-me will listen to a sermon and be gripped by its truth. As the preacher declares, *"For God has not given us a spirit of fear and timidity, but of power, love, and self-discipline"* (2 Timothy 1:7). I want to fist-pump the air, high-five my neighbour and shout "Amen!" I'm excited about the courage and love, the strong will and determination the Lord has given me. But however excited rocky-soil-me was on Sunday, that truth has evaporated by Monday when I visit my doctor, who has another "truth" to tell me. Suddenly fear takes over. I am no longer fist pumping about my spirit of power, I am hand wringing, feeling anxious and fearful that I have a weak body. I have an attack of spiritual amnesia and forget the truth I'd previously embraced. Rocky-soil-me looks in fear at what the future might hold, but forgets who really holds the future. Rocky-soil-me welcomes truth that comes from the Lord, but allows it to be overshadowed by the "truth" that comes from others.

So what about the "thorny soil person"? This is the person who hears and temporarily accepts God's Word, but allows it to be crowded out by the plentiful supply of distractions and worries of life. Have you ever popped into a mega supermarket when you only really needed one item? All you needed was a pint of milk, but you are distracted as you pass row upon row of "must-have" items. Before long, the hand basket you came in with is too heavy and you need to swap it for a trolley, and by the time you get to the checkout, your trolley is fully loaded! This is like the worries that bombard thorny-soil-me. Numerous thoughts and distractions keep getting added to our "basket" until we can no longer carry them all. Overwhelmed with anxiety we collapse under life's pressures, as if we will never be able to push through the challenges. Truth is simply squashed by the pressure of life.

Thorny-soil-me forgets the promise that Paul spoke when he said, *"Don't worry about anything; instead, pray about everything. Tell God what you need, and thank him for all he has done. Then you will experience God's peace, which exceeds anything we can understand. His peace will guard your hearts and minds as you live in Christ Jesus"* (Philippians 4:6-7).

Then Jesus brings us hope when He speaks of a different kind of soil – a "good soil person", which represents, *"those who hear and accept God's word and produce a harvest"* (Mark 4:20). We learn that hearing must be followed by action. Just to hear is not enough. Rather, God's Word must be heard, accepted, believed and understood, received and put into practice. Hearing and accepting truth takes it deeper into our Spirit, so that the enemy can't snatch it away. Hearing and accepting truth means that we begin to practice it, so it can't simply be forgotten. Hearing and accepting truth means that we keep our focus and we don't get distracted or overwhelmed.

James explains this beautifully when he says,

"Don't just listen to God's word. You must do what it says. Otherwise, you are only fooling yourselves. For if you listen to the word and don't obey, it is like glancing at your face in a mirror. You see yourself, walk away, and forget what you look like. But if you look carefully into the perfect law that sets you free, and if you do what it says and don't forget what you heard, then God will bless you for doing it." (James 1:22-25)

It is in the Word of God that we find fresh revelation of Jesus.

Through Him we can hear His Word, do what it says, and become fruitful in increasing measure. Good-soil-me remains in Christ and through Him I will bear much fruit.

Meditate on this:

"Guard your heart above all else, for it determines the course of your life." (Proverbs 4:23)

Going deeper still:

What condition do you consider your heart to be in right now? How does it match up to the four different types of person represented by the soil? What steps can you take to protect the truth planted in you, to deepen the soil and clear away the thorns, so that your heart can be more like the good soil?

Let's pray...

Lord, please forgive me that I allow so many distractions and doubts to crowd in and rob me of your truth. Please help me to hold tight to what I know by holding tight to who I know – you! Help me to remain in you and allow your truth to remain in me, that I might be fruitful. Amen.

DAY 13:
GROWING IN THE DARK

————•————

"Your word is a lamp to guide my feet and a light for my path."
(Psalm 119:105)

Before we move onto the next stage of our journey together we will spend one more day considering who we are rooted in.

I know that Jesus said He was the vine and we are the branches, but for today we're going to imagine that He is the soil in which we're rooted. Our roots are plunging deep into His truth, as our shoots are reaching towards His grace and light. Stay with me, there is some wisdom to be gleaned…

There is something fascinating about the way plants are created to have both a gravitational attraction and a pull towards the light. The ability for a plant to respond to external stimuli is called tropism. So a plant can grow in response to gravity with gravitropism and in response to light with phototropism. A hormone called auxin, when distributed evenly throughout a stem, enables all sides of the stem to grow at the same rate, enabling the plant to grow towards the light, away from gravity. At the risk of making you think you are back in Biology class at school, stick with this, it's interesting!

If a plant is tipped on its side, the auxin will concentrate itself on the lower side of the stem – which causes the lower side to elongate, so that the stem can grow upwards again, reaching for the light.

Wait, there's more! Roots can do something similar, just in the opposite way. A plant's roots will change direction when it is tipped on its side. The auxin concentrates on the roots' lower sides, inhibiting elongation of root growth, which makes the upper side grow longer – thereby turning the root back downward into the soil!

Come on, admit it, that's an amazing design! There's still one more fact to consider. Roots not only change direction if a plant is tipped over, they also change direction if they encounter a dense object such as a rock. In this case, the auxin will focus on the lower side of the roots, enabling them to find a pathway around the rock so that normal growth can be resumed.

Think about this: If God can design plants with this incredible capacity, just consider what might be possible for us! Have you ever felt like one of those roots? Things are going well in your life and you're making progress, when suddenly you bump into a massive, rock-like obstacle. Or you feel like life has suddenly tipped you up and you think your position has been changed forever. Consider yourself to be a root and a shoot! What do you gravitate towards? What are you reaching for?

Unfortunately, we all have an inbuilt human tendency to gravitate towards sin. We enjoy sin. After all, we aren't going to be tempted by something that doesn't look good, at least on the surface.

"The Lord observed the extent of human wickedness on the earth, and he saw that everything they thought or imagined was consistently and totally evil." (Genesis 6:5)

Yet the Lord's desire for every single one of us is to reach out to Him.

"His purpose was for the nations to seek after God and perhaps feel their way toward Him and find Him – though he is not far from

any one of us. For in Him we live and move and exist." (Acts 17:27-28a)

The Lord is so close and calling us to pursue Him – to reach to the light and to draw down into His rich depth.

Sometimes we do feel like we've been "tipped" by life and we're in a challenging and uncomfortable position. Then there are the obstacles that seem to block our path at every turn, prohibiting our progress. But just as God designed roots and shoots in such a way that they can receive the nutrients they need and grow towards the light, He will take of us. How much more grace and provision is available to help you grow in truth towards His light? You can "grow past" obstacles and beyond challenges. No tipping point is too far that we cannot still grow in His truth. We can even grow during the dark times and still come out fruitful.

Friend, there are going to be rocks ahead of us all. Life will tip us. But we don't have to stop at these obstacles. Jesus said, *"If you had faith even as small as a mustard seed, you could say to this mountain, 'Move from here to there,' and it would move. Nothing would be impossible"* (Matthew 17:20).

We don't have to be defeated in the "tipping". Rather, like the roots of plants, we can keep growing and reach beyond.

There was a time when Jacob was wrestling with God and experiencing more than a little tipping, yet in that moment he clung on saying, *"I will not let you go unless you bless me"* (Genesis 32:26). There has never been a better time to determine that you will cling on to God; to reach for Him and allow Him to help you move beyond the "rocks" and the "tipping".

There are numerous examples in the Bible. If David had been put off by Goliath the Israelites would have been defeated. Instead, he knew the Lord was bigger than the obstacle he faced. If Joshua and Caleb had adopted the views of the others in the spying party, they would have been held back by the thought of the giants in the land and missed the fertile grapes! Don't be limited by the obstacles you see before you. Look beyond them to where your hope comes from.

As we conclude this section of our devotional we remind ourselves of the all-important truth: roots matter. This is about the who and not the what. As our eyes focus on the Lord, as we remain in Him, as we allow His truth to saturate us, so we will become fruitful.

Remain in Him. Move towards Him today and know that He is (and will always be) enough.

Meditate on this:
"Each time he said, 'My grace is all you need. My power works best in weakness.' So now I am glad to boast about my weaknesses, so that the power of Christ can work through me." (2 Corinthians 12:9)

Going Deeper Still:
Imagine again being a root finding its way in the dark. What is blocking you from reaching deeper into truth? What rocks and rubble do you need to "grow beyond"? How can you grow in truth in spite of obstacles?

Let's pray...
Lord, please help me to see things as you see things. Help me to not be put off by obstacles, but to see that you are bigger than any obstacle. Lord, help me to remain in you always. Amen.

Section 2

KNOWING THE GARDENER

"I am the true grapevine, and my Father is the gardener. He cuts off every branch of mine that doesn't produce fruit, and he prunes the branches that do bear fruit so they will produce even more."
(John 15:1-2)

DAY 14:
WHO HOLDS THE SECATEURS?

"O Lord, your unfailing love fills the earth; teach me your decrees."
(Psalm 119:64)

We've been looking at the roots, now we're going to turn our gaze on the Gardener. As we come into this next stage of our journey of growing in fruitfulness, we turn to look at pruning! Pruning never seems pleasant, and the thought of the pain it might involve might make you want to skip this section so we can continue talking about fruit. But I urge you to stick with the process. Stay the course – there is so much to discover that will help you.

Plants are pruned for multiple reasons. Already fruitful plants/trees need to be pruned because of the potential they have for an even greater yield. Other branches are trimmed because they no longer show signs of life. Whatever the reason for the pruning, our focus remains on who is doing the pruning, rather than what is being pruned.

Jesus made it clear that pruning is part of our growth in Him:

"I am the true grapevine, and my Father is the gardener. He cuts off every branch of mine that doesn't produce fruit, and he prunes the branches that do bear fruit so they will produce even more." (John 15:1-2)

Our heavenly Father is the Gardener and the one who does the pruning.

When my youngest daughter was little she loved playing outdoors by the flower beds with a little watering can in hand, feeding the plants, playing in the mud, and picking up clumps of grass (as well as the occasional earthworm). She loved "gardening". However, if I had sent her out into the garden with a pair of secateurs and told her to prune the plants, the garden would have been decimated, hacked about. Plants would have been enthusiastically but ignorantly chopped, flourishing buds dismembered from their stems. The result would have looked more like a massacre than a prune. In the hands of a small child, pruning shears would cause damage, not promote growth.

However, put the secateurs into the hands of an expert gardener – one who knows and loves plants – and the sharp edged shears would move swiftly, calmly, carefully. Every cut would be precise, intended for the purpose of bettering the garden and increasing the eventual fruitfulness of the plants.

Our Father – the Gardener – is the same Father who, *"loved the world so much that he gave his only Son so that anyone who believes in him shall not perish but have eternal life"* (John 3:16 TLB).

The same loving Gardener desires to prune us in such a way that our sins are removed and we become fruitful.

"The Lord is compassionate and merciful, slow to get angry and filled with unfailing love. He will not constantly accuse us, nor remain angry forever. He does not punish us for all our sins; he does not deal harshly with us, as we deserve. For his unfailing love toward those who fear him is as great as the height of the heavens above the earth. He has removed our sins as far from us as the east is from the west. The Lord is like a father to his children, tender and compassionate to those who fear him." (Psalm 103:8-13)

If we are the branches in the hands of the Gardener, we can be confident that He knows what He is doing. In the hands of the Creator, the created are shaped and reshaped for their good, for a bigger purpose.

None of us would admit to really enjoying those seasons in life where the Father's pruning and discipline bring a cutting edge to our comfort. The feeling of being cut back and restricted is uncomfortable, and often painful. During those times, if we remember who holds the secateurs and is shaping our life, we gain an important perspective.

Many years ago I ran a child-minding business in our family home. It seemed the perfect way to be able to look after my own children whilst bringing in some much needed money. There were times when our home was full to bursting with after-school children. All of the children had to abide by some general house rules that kept everyone safe and encouraged mutual respect. But I had higher expectations of my children than I did of my paying "guests". For example, I couldn't insist that a "borrowed child" I was looking after do their homework after school, but I could insist that mine did! From nap-taking to turn-taking it was always slightly different for a "borrowed child" and an "own child". Certain behaviours can be overlooked in children who are handed back to their parents at the end of the day – but not my own, simply because they were mine!

In the same way, the Bible speaks of how God takes a special interest in His own children. The writer of Hebrews speaks about it this way:

"My child, don't make light of the Lord's discipline, and don't give up when He corrects you. For the Lord disciplines those He loves, and He punishes each one he accepts as His child. As you endure this divine discipline, remember that God is treating you as His own children. Who ever heard of a child who is never disciplined by its

father? If God doesn't discipline you as He does all of his children, it means that you are illegitimate and are not really his children at all. Since we respected our earthly fathers who disciplined us, shouldn't we submit even more to the discipline of the Father of our spirits, and live forever? For our earthly fathers disciplined us for a few years, doing the best they knew how. But God's discipline is always good for us, so that we might share in His holiness. No discipline is enjoyable while it is happening – it's painful! But afterward there will be a peaceful harvest of right living for those who are trained in this way." (Hebrews 12:5-11)

Pruning at the hands of our loving Gardener, our Heavenly Father, always produces a harvest of fruitfulness. How reassuring that our Father doesn't expect us to grow by ourselves into perfection. Rather, He lovingly helps us, shapes us and nurture us, imperfect and stunted though we may be. This is good news!

Meditate on this:
"My child, don't reject the Lord's discipline, and don't be upset when He corrects you. For the Lord corrects those He loves, just as a father corrects a child in whom He delights." (Proverbs 3:11-12)

Going deeper still:
How have you experienced the love of the Lord through pruning – in a way that has brought about a greater maturity and a closer relationship between you and your heavenly Father?

Let's pray…
Lord, please help me today not to focus so much on what might be pruned, but on you. You are both my loving Father and the Gardener. Please help me to see you more and know your love more in the experiences of my day. Amen.

DAY 15:
STIRRING IN STUFF

———•———

"I am your servant; deal with me in unfailing love, and teach me your decrees."
(Psalm 119:124)

We have a tiny little fig tree growing in our front garden, which was cut from a mature tree once owned by a friend. In previous years our family has benefited from the delicious fruit harvested from the parent plant. Those figs really were delicious – so sweet they almost tasted too good to be healthy! I am not surprised that Jesus enjoyed eating figs when He was travelling around. They are super-loaded with nutrients when ripened by the Galilean sun. Delicious!

So here is an interesting fact about figs: they have an eye on their environment! Figs grow on a Ficus Tree and are unique in having an opening called an ostiole or "eye". This helps the figs "communicate" with their environment, which enhances their development.

However, there was one fig tree that I'm sure "didn't see it coming" when Jesus walked by it one day. This particular tree wasn't producing any fruit, so there were no figs on it when Jesus wanted something to eat and He "cursed" the tree.

"The next morning as they were leaving Bethany, Jesus was hungry. He noticed a fig tree in full leaf a little way off, so he went

over to see if he could find any figs. But there were only leaves because it was too early in the season for fruit. Then Jesus said to the tree, 'May no one ever eat your fruit again!' And the disciples heard him say it." (Mark 11:12-14)

To understand this story we should consider the wider context and symbolism, otherwise it may appear particularly harsh. Just before this incident, Jesus had made His triumphal entry into Jerusalem on the back of a donkey. Large crowds of people had gathered, watching and praising Him as He passed. It was as if the people in the crowd were praising Him because they realised He really was King. Everything seemed good, celebratory, full of faith and life.

But however things appeared at that moment, Jesus knew it was too early for people to really understand what His kingship meant. They praised Him at the parade, but Jesus knew they would abandon Him at the cross. Things were not as they appeared on the surface. So when Jesus spotted a green leafed yet fruitless fig tree, He took the opportunity to use it as an illustration of the reality of hypocrisy.

Historically, the fig tree was used as a metaphor for Israel. And while green leaves can make a tree appear healthy, it is only the fruit which is the real evidence of its health. Jesus knew that Israel was not healthy at that time, despite appearances.

Jesus is always looking for fruitfulness in His followers. He doesn't just want "green leaves" – the appearance of health. Rather He desires His disciples to live fruitful lives from root to tip. Jesus is not interested in the superficial adoration of people paying lip service to Him in the moment. He looks for those who love Him from their hearts. As we know, healthy fruit comes from healthy roots.

With Jesus, it is possible for us to bear fruit constantly, whatever the season. Such is His power in our lives. In Luke's gospel there is another fig tree story which takes this understanding to a whole new level. Here we can learn something fresh about the heart of the Lord and His desire for our fruitfulness:

"Then Jesus told this story: A man planted a fig tree in his garden and came again and again to see if there was any fruit on it, but he was always disappointed. Finally, he said to his gardener, 'I've waited three years, and there hasn't been a single fig! Cut it down. It's just taking up space in the garden.' The gardener answered, 'Sir, give it one more chance. Leave it another year, and I'll give it special attention and plenty of fertiliser. If we get figs next year, fine. If not, then you can cut it down.'" (Luke 13:6-9)

The implication of the parable is that Jesus expects His disciples to bear fruit within a reasonable period of time, and if they don't, something is wrong! But notice also the message of grace in the parable. The gardener, in this instance representing Jesus Himself, offers to give his personal attention to the tree and apply plenty of fertiliser.

I need to watch my language here, but you know there are some things in life that really stink. And when bad stuff happens, people will talk about it hitting the fan, if you catch my drift! The question I find myself asking is this: when the bad stuff of life gets thrown in our direction, will we trust the Lord to use it for our growth; to bring about fruitfulness in our lives? Will we trust Him to use it to nourish our roots in Him? To cause us to grow better not bitter, stronger not harder? Will we trust Him with the details of our lives so that we become more "nutritious" to those around us?

We were not put on this earth simply to take up space, but to add our distinct, flavoursome fruit. Like the little figs with their "eyes" on their environment, the Lord longs for us to keep our eyes on Him, with our roots embedded in His truth; allowing life's rich experiences to move us to draw everything we need from Him. Jesus longs to give you "special attention", but this might not come without "plenty of fertiliser"!

Many years ago I thought my whole future was over when I didn't get the A-Level results required for my chosen next steps. Everything I thought had been planned for my career path was suddenly over. Instead, I was forced into a year out with intensive studies, the resitting of exams and getting some work experience. In the midst of all of this, I entered into a year of "special attention", focusing on the Lord and seeking His will. Whilst it initially seemed to me that the stuff had hit the proverbial fan, the Lord used this time to strengthen and equip me for my future. More than that, I found my path being completely redirected. I ended up going to a different city, studying for a different degree. There in Norwich, I connected with people who shaped my future, not least my husband, Tim. I thought it had all gone wrong, but God was upgrading my destiny. My failure became a success in the hands of the Lord.

Notice in Jesus' parable that fruit from the intensive fertiliser treatment was not expected immediately. But the gardener fully expected to see a difference within a year. Take courage – things won't be the same next year when Jesus is at work!

Meditate on this:

"You didn't choose me. I chose you. I appointed you to go and produce lasting fruit, so that the Father will give you whatever you ask for, using my name. This is my command: Love each other." (John 15:16-17)

Going deeper still:

What "stuff" is going on in your life for which you've not yet discovered God's truth? What would it look like for you to experience Jesus' special attention in this matter? How can the people around you help you grow and how can you help those around you to also grow?

Let's pray...

Lord, please forgive me for the areas of my life that have not been fruitful when you would have wanted them to be. Lord, will you help me to allow you to use all the stuff in my life to draw me closer to you – to find your truth in my circumstances? Help me to rely on your care and teaching, so that I might produce the fruit in my life that you desire. Amen.

DAY 16:
DORMANT POTENTIAL

———•———

"Keep me from lying to myself; give me the privilege of knowing
your instructions."
(Psalm 119:29)

Consider a seed which is planted into soil. If the seed is going to become fruitful it cannot remain unchanged. To release its latent energy – the seed's dormant potential – oxygen, light, water and temperature must converge in the most conducive arrangement to bring about change.

When seeds imbibe (draw up) water in the right temperature and conditions, the enzymes and food supplies become hydrated giving them the energy to grow. The radical (root) is the first part to be seen breaking through the seed shell, followed by the shoot. All this activity is taking place in the dark depths, before a seed's shoot emerges above the soil line. For a seed to produce a plant, the change is continuous. The bottom line is: it cannot remain unchanged or self-contained. It needs water and it needs to be broken.

Jesus used this analogy when talking to His disciples about His own death. He gave them a glimpse of what they could expect in the future.

"I tell you the truth, unless a kernel of wheat is planted in the soil and dies, it remains alone. But its death will produce many new

kernels – a plentiful harvest of new lives. Those who love their life in this world will lose it. Those who care nothing for their life in this world will keep it for eternity. Anyone who wants to serve me must follow me, because my servants must be where I am. And the Father will honour anyone who serves me." (John 12:24-26)

Jesus challenged His disciples, explaining that to follow Him meant having a new set of priorities for their lives. They were to deny, even die to, themselves for His sake, for His cause:

"Then Jesus said to his disciples, 'If any of you wants to be my follower, you must give up your selfish ways, take up your cross, and follow me. If you try to hang on to your life, you will lose it. But if you give up your life for my sake, you will save it.'" (Matthew 16:24-25)

In Jesus' "pruning economy" it becomes apparent that gain comes from loss! Giving up the right to control our own life enables us to gain eternal life with Him. Giving up the right to hold on to the "fruit" on our "branches" enables us to receive even more from the Father, in His time.

Listen to how Jesus explained to His disciples about the cost of following Him:

"As they were walking along, someone said to Jesus, 'I will follow you wherever you go.' But Jesus replied, 'Foxes have dens to live in, and birds have nests, but the Son of Man has no place even to lay His head.' He said to another person, 'Come, follow me.' The man agreed, but he said, 'Lord, first let me return home and bury my father.' But Jesus told him, 'Let the spiritually dead bury their own dead! Your duty is to go and preach about the Kingdom of God.' Another said, 'Yes, Lord, I will follow you, but first let me say goodbye to my family.' But Jesus told him, 'Anyone who puts a hand to the plough and then looks back is not fit for the Kingdom of God.'" (Luke 9:57-62)

On face value this passage is a little uncomfortable to read as Jesus uses three cameos to explain the cost of following Him.

Firstly, Jesus was living an itinerant lifestyle, moving from place to place. If someone was going to follow Him then there would be times of sleeping on wild hillsides, not in a warm home. Following Jesus was not a lifestyle choice that promoted the comfort of the follower!

In the Jewish context in which Jesus spoke it was the eldest son's responsibility to deal with the family estate in the event of their parents' death, and to ensure the burial occurred within twenty-four hours of the death. This meant there was an immediate flurry of activity from the eldest son when a father died. This potential Christ-follower was in the crowd listening to Jesus though – not at home making funeral arrangements. So although he requested time to bury his father, he could have been gone a long time, because the implication is that is father isn't dead yet. In other words, instead of being ready to follow Jesus there and then, the man really wanted to head home and live his life for a bit – He would come back and follow Jesus when it was a bit more convenient! This is not wholehearted discipleship. It's not true follower-ship. It's not seeking the Lord first. This man had his own agenda in mind. Jesus invited the man to delegate his responsibilities as eldest son to someone else (perhaps another brother), rather than waiting for the father to die. Whatever potential he had to bear fruit that would bring life to others, he was unwilling to sacrifice his comfort. He didn't want to plant his seed and entrust his life to Christ.

The final cameo in this conversation is about a farmer ploughing a field. Now, my field-ploughing experience is limited as I grew up in a suburban hotel not a farmstead in the shires! However, even I know that looking forward is the only way to plough in a straight line! Jesus was explaining to the potential follower that to be moving forward whilst looking backwards was not going to be possible. For growth to happen forwards, the focus cannot be backward.

For a seed to become fruitful there is a cost which involves both changes and brokenness – and it is the same with following Jesus. What needs to be sown today? What comforts need to be given up for the sake of your future? As with the early disciples, the cost of following Jesus means that our comfort is not to be our focus, but rather His purposes. Our potential is only realised when we die to self so that we can live.

Meditate on this:

"But forget all that – it is nothing compared to what I am going to do. For I am about to do something new. See, I have already begun! Do you not see it? I will make a pathway through the wilderness. I will create rivers in the dry wasteland." (Isaiah 43:18-19)

Going deeper:

What might you have to let go of, change focus away from, or reprioritise in order to move forward with Christ?

Let's pray...

Lord, help me to be a disciple who is to be willing to live outside my comfort zone, have my priorities re-ordered, and to keep my eyes fixed on you. Amen.

DAY 17:
HIM FIRST

————·————

"I will hurry, without delay, to obey your commands."
(Psalm 119:60)

Let's be honest, in our fast-paced culture with our busy lives there are just so many things that demand our attention. Life is complicated with myriad choices requiring urgent responses. Walk down any high street and banks are competing to loan us money. Restaurants are competing to fill our stomachs. Coffee shops are competing to give us a caffeine fix. Retailers are competing to get us to wear their brands. And that is just a simple walk down the high street! Not to mention the "digital high street" with the demands of social media. Or the demands for our time that come from being connected to family, our community, student-life, work-life, church-life, or whole-life! It's exhausting just thinking about it all.

Often, so many options are open to us that we can struggle to make a choice. Others struggle to accept the consequences once they've made a decision. Cognitive dissonance arises when we're inconsistent and lacking in confidence over the decisions we've made, and we battle regrets over possible wrong choices. Buyer's remorse is a pandemic.

There's a new name for this remorse, coined by those younger than me: FOMO – The Fear of Missing Out! Making one decision about how to spend our time or money means denying another option. It means missing out on something, and the pressure builds with the threat of possible rejection.

These emotional responses to the demands for our attention can cause a huge amount of stress, anxiety and worry. Jesus didn't use the expression FOMO, but He fully appreciated the inner conflict that can tie everyone in knots. He said,

"That is why I tell you not to worry about everyday life – whether you have enough food and drink, or enough clothes to wear. Isn't life more than food, and your body more than clothing? Look at the birds. They don't plant or harvest or store food in barns, for your heavenly Father feeds them. And aren't you far more valuable to him than they are? Can all your worries add a single moment to your life? 'And why worry about your clothing? Look at the lilies of the field and how they grow. They don't work or make their clothing, yet Solomon in all his glory was not dressed as beautifully as they are. And if God cares so wonderfully for wildflowers that are here today and thrown into the fire tomorrow, he will certainly care for you. Why do you have so little faith? So don't worry about these things, saying, 'What will we eat? What will we drink? What will we wear?' These things dominate the thoughts of unbelievers, but your heavenly Father already knows all your needs. Seek the Kingdom of God above all else, and live righteously, and he will give you everything you need. So don't worry about tomorrow, for tomorrow will bring its own worries. Today's trouble is enough for today." (Matthew 6:25-34)

When we take our eyes off our needs and fix them firmly on the Lord (the one who really knows our needs), we can begin to let go of the stress of buyer's remorse and FOMO. When we focus on the one who knows what we really need – and who will meet those needs – we can grow in confidence that all of our *real* needs will be met in His perfect time.

Isaiah spoke about this, challenging the people of God to turn to Him for their help, as fruitful blessing would follow the barrenness of suffering. The Lord was ready then, as He is now, to draw so close that we can hear His voice of direction. God comes so close to us that even if He whispers, we won't miss it. He comes close when we ask for His help.

"So the Lord must wait for you to come to him so he can show you his love and compassion. For the Lord is a faithful God. Blessed are those who wait for his help. O people of Zion, who live in Jerusalem, you will weep no more. He will be gracious if you ask for help. He will surely respond to the sound of your cries. Though the Lord gave you adversity for food and suffering for drink, he will still be with you to teach you. You will see your teacher with your own eyes. Your own ears will hear him. Right behind you a voice will say, 'This is the way you should go,' whether to the right or to the left. Then you will destroy all your silver idols and your precious gold images. You will throw them out like filthy rags, saying to them, 'Good riddance!' Then the Lord will bless you with rain at planting time. There will be wonderful harvests and plenty of pastureland for your livestock." (Isaiah 30:18-23)

Even with the encouragement to "seek the Kingdom of God above all else" there is a tension we will experience. "Seeking" is not the same as "seeing"! In our journey towards fruitfulness, as we trust ourselves to the Gardener for His care, we should understand that sometimes we will hear the Lord's voice behind us. This means we won't always be able to see Him leading from in front of us. Sometimes when we struggle with choices and direction in life, and we feel we can't "see" the Lord in our circumstances, perhaps it's because we need to quieten ourselves to listen instead.

Seeking God first means sorting our priorities. The things that the people of God found so important to themselves were seen as idols by the Lord. Seeking Him first meant that His people were no longer lured by the pull of idols. Rather they could willingly say, "Good riddance."

If the promise of God's presence and guidance is as real to us as it was to the Israelites, then surely so too is the need for us to say "good riddance" to all the clutter and distractions that grab our focus; the modern day idols that shout for our loyalty. What if our FOMO became FOMOOH – The Fear of Missing Out on Him! What if we focused first on the Lord, not wanting to miss anything He has for us?

Asking the Lord for help, choosing Him first and allowing ourselves to be planted in Him will cause fruitfulness to follow the challenges we have faced.

Meditate on this:
"Trust in the Lord with all your heart; do not depend on your own understanding. Seek his will in all you do, and he will show you which path to take." (Proverbs 3:5-6)

Going deeper still:
In what ways can you ask God for help? What guidance are you looking for? Are there ways in which you can put God first? Do you need to say "good riddance" to anything today, before you can move on?

Let's pray…
Lord, I thank you that your Word tells me you want to answer me when I call for help, and that you will come close to me. Lord, help me get rid of anything that comes between you and me, so that I might clearly hear your voice and know your presence. Amen.

DAY 18:
LESS FOR MORE

—————

"You are good and do only good; teach me your decrees."
(Psalm 119:68)

Neither my husband nor I are particularly green fingered. However, we do occasionally potter around the garden. The problem is, we don't prioritise our time to do this regularly enough for the garden to benefit. If we want our garden to be full of beautiful flowers, then we will need to tend it regularly. But we seem to put our time into other activities and, as a result, our garden is not blessed with much beauty! We do, however, have some vines which my husband planted and nurtures, every now and then. One year, other priorities took over and he went to look at the vines after a longer break than usual, to discover they were not in good shape. Looking as if they were dead, Tim made the drastic decision to go for a full-on prune back. It was the last hope for their survival. Seriously, this vine was pruned within an inch of its life, right down near the base of the stem! But amazingly, by the end of the season, the vines produced a greater crop than we'd seen before.

The book of Job is all about pruning. We read of a man who was known as, *"blameless – a man of complete integrity. He feared God and stayed away from evil"* (Job 1:1). Job was a very wealthy and fruitful man who owned donkeys, sheep, oxen and camels, and had many servants. In addition he was the patriarch of a large family with seven sons and three daughters. Job enjoyed a favoured and fruitful life in every way.

However, the enemy accused God of putting a protective shield around Job, and raised the complaint that Job was only obedient to God because his life was "easy". God knew otherwise. He knew that Job loved Him not because of what the Lord gave him, but because of who the Lord was. So He allowed Job to be tested. Over time, the severity of the test escalated and Job's life was pruned on a significant scale. Through enemy attacks Job lost his oxen, donkeys, camels and his servants. Through fire he lost his sheep. Job lost all his children in a tragic tornado. Within a short period of time, everything in his life that looked like healthy fruitfulness was gone – completely destroyed! Then God allowed Job's health to suffer too, with sores and boils. He suffered excruciatingly.

Note that the Lord didn't send the sickness or cause the attacks. He did, however, allow them. Such was the Lord's confidence in Job's love for Him – love for who He was, not what He gave him. Seeing further than any scheme of the enemy the Lord knew that, not only would He be glorified, but in the end Job would be even more blessed … in the end!

A dramatic and prolonged season of lament unfolds as Job comes to wish he had never been born. Sadness and sorrow consumed him. However, he never sinned against God. As much as he complained about his life, he didn't blame the Lord or turn his back on Him. Rather, he knew that the Lord remained the living God, sovereign in all His ways.

By the end of the story the situation became clear, even to Job's doubting friends:

"...the Lord restored his fortunes. In fact, the Lord gave him twice as much as before!" (Job 42:10)

The Lord brought about an incredible restoration in Job's life. We read that, *"the Lord blessed Job in the second half of his life even more than in the beginning"* (Job 42:12).

Jesus knew the benefits of pruning. He said, *"I am the true grapevine, and my Father is the gardener. He cuts off every branch of mine that doesn't produce fruit, and he prunes the branches that do bear fruit so they will produce even more."* (John 15:1-2)

On another occasion Jesus spoke to His disciples about having a heart willing to be pruned:

"Then Jesus said to his disciples, 'I tell you the truth, it is very hard for a rich person to enter the Kingdom of Heaven. I'll say it again – it is easier for a camel to go through the eye of a needle than for a rich person to enter the Kingdom of God!' The disciples were astounded. 'Then who in the world can be saved?' they asked. Jesus looked at them intently and said, 'Humanly speaking, it is impossible. But with God everything is possible.' Then Peter said to him, 'We've given up everything to follow you. What will we get?' Jesus replied, 'I assure you that when the world is made new and the Son of Man sits upon his glorious throne, you who have been my followers will also sit on twelve thrones, judging the twelve tribes of Israel. And everyone who has given up houses or brothers or sisters or father or mother or children or property, for my sake, will receive a hundred times as much in return and will inherit eternal life. But many who are the greatest now will be least important then, and those who seem least important now will be the greatest then." (Matthew 19:23-30)

This a powerful teaching. We see very clearly that in God's economy, less is more. The apostle John understood this principle as he wrote in one of his letters,

"Do not love this world nor the things it offers you, for when you love the world, you do not have the love of the Father in you. For

the world offers only a craving for physical pleasure, a craving for everything we see, and pride in our achievements and possessions. These are not from the Father, but are from this world. And this world is fading away, along with everything that people crave. But anyone who does what pleases God will live forever." (1 John 2:15-17)

Loving the Lord for who He is rather than what He gives us will open up our life to be pruned. We can allow our cravings for comforts and pleasures to be overtaken by our love for the Father. As we grow in our desire to live Kingdom-focused lives, willing to settle for less of the things of this world so that Christ becomes our all in all, we discover that less is indeed more.

Meditate on this:

"And now, Israel, what does the Lord your God require of you? He requires only that you fear the Lord your God, and live in a way that pleases him, and love him and serve him with all your heart and soul." (Deuteronomy 10:12)

Going deeper still:

In what ways can you love God even in the tests that you face? Remember a time when you came through a test and found yourself closer to Him and more blessed. How can you gain strength for your current situation from the tests you went through before?

Let's pray...

Lord, help me to love you for who you are, not what you give me. Lord, may I be so confident in who you are that I will grow in the certainty of your love and presence being with me at all times. Amen.

DAY 19:
FRUITFUL ATTITUDES

———•———

"O Lord, your unfailing love fills the earth; teach me your decrees."
(Psalm 119:64)

Many years ago in my English Literature class at school I read a book which, whilst I would eventually learn to love it, initially baffled me. In my mind, the author seemed unable to make his mind up about what he was describing. Here's an extract of what I read:

"It was the best of times, it was the worst of times, it was the age of wisdom, it was the age of foolishness, it was the epoch of belief, it was the epoch of incredulity, it was the season of Light, it was the season of Darkness, it was the spring of hope, it was the winter of despair, we had everything before us, we had nothing before us, we were all going direct to Heaven, we were all going direct the other way – in short, the period was so far like the present period, that some of its noisiest authorities insisted on its being received, for good or for evil, in the superlative degree of comparison only."

This is how Charles Dickens opens his classic novel, *A Tale of Two Cities*. As I grappled with the apparent contradictions in the text above, I nearly missed the whole point: Dickens was describing two cities.

Similarly the Kingdom of Earth and the Kingdom of God are

so different, yet sometimes we miss the distinctions. Time and again Jesus turned human reality on its head as He revealed His greater reality. The audience present at one of Jesus' most famous sermons were perhaps as confused by what He had to say as I was by Dickens. His speech seemed full of contradictions, as if He was describing two distinct states of existence. Speaking about everyday earthly struggles, Jesus spoke of unlikely heavenly outcomes:

"God blesses those who are poor and realise their need for him, for the Kingdom of Heaven is theirs. God blesses those who mourn, for they will be comforted. God blesses those who are humble, for they will inherit the whole earth. God blesses those who hunger and thirst for justice, for they will be satisfied. God blesses those who are merciful, for they will be shown mercy. God blesses those whose hearts are pure, for they will see God. God blesses those who work for peace, for they will be called the children of God. God blesses those who are persecuted for doing right, for the Kingdom of Heaven is theirs. God blesses you when people mock you and persecute you and lie about you and say all sorts of evil things against you because you are my followers. Be happy about it! Be very glad! For a great reward awaits you in heaven. And remember, the ancient prophets were persecuted in the same way." (Matthew 5:1-12)

Being blessed in a season of lack or loss seems an unlikely contradiction. However, it is in acknowledging our lack of ability to meet our own needs (honest poverty) that we are able to reach out in dependence on our Heavenly Father and see true value. When we admit our bankruptcy we discover real riches. The more we rely on and draw closer to Him, the more we will know the provision of His presence. Being rooted into our Provider God, we can enjoy the fruit of His provision.

As Paul said,

"I know how to live on almost nothing or with everything. I have learned the secret of living in every situation, whether it is with a full stomach or empty, with plenty or little. For I can do everything through Christ, who gives me strength." (Philippians 4:12-13)

He had learned that what matters is not what he could provide for himself, but who he could depend on for his provision.

It is only when we have known loss and grief that we truly know what comfort is. Before loss, comfort is merely a theory, much like a meal on a menu that's not yet been tasted. In knowing grief we know what it is to dig deep into the presence of the Lord and allow His hope to live within us.

As Paul wrote to the Thessalonians,

"And now, dear brothers and sisters, we want you to know what will happen to the believers who have died so you will not grieve like people who have no hope. For since we believe that Jesus died and was raised to life again, we also believe that when Jesus returns, God will bring back with him the believers who have died." (1 Thessalonians 4:13-14)

What a way to live, with the fruit of the contentment of God's provision being borne out of a season of poverty; the fruit of comfort and hope borne out of a season of loss.

In knowing our weaknesses we can begin to grow fruitful in strength. As Jesus said,

"Healthy people don't need a doctor – sick people do. I have come to call not those who think they are righteous, but those who know they are sinners and need to repent." (Luke 5:31-32)

Paul understood what it was to live a life of contradictions. He lived with an unidentified "thorn" and embraced his own weakness. He did not celebrate his weakness or indulge in self-pity, but rather recognised that when he was no longer self-reliant, the Lord could reveal Himself most profoundly.

"I will boast only about my weaknesses. If I wanted to boast, I would be no fool in doing so, because I would be telling the truth. But I won't do it, because I don't want anyone to give me credit beyond what they can see in my life or hear in my message, even though I have received such wonderful revelations from God. So to keep me from becoming proud, I was given a thorn in my flesh, a messenger from Satan to torment me and keep me from becoming proud. Three different times I begged the Lord to take it away. Each time he said, 'My grace is all you need. My power works best in weakness.' So now I am glad to boast about my weaknesses, so that the power of Christ can work through me. That's why I take pleasure in my weaknesses, and in the insults, hardships, persecutions, and troubles that I suffer for Christ. For when I am weak, then I am strong." (2 Corinthians 12:5-10)

So today, as we live in and for the Kingdom of God, with its sharp contrast to this broken world, we too can say that in our worst of times we can know the Lord's best. In our foolishness, we can know the Lord's wisdom. In seasons of darkness we can know the Lord's light.

Meditate on this:

"Dear brothers and sisters, when troubles of any kind come your way, consider it an opportunity for great joy. For you know that when your faith is tested, your endurance has a chance to grow. So let it grow, for when your endurance is fully developed, you will be perfect and complete, needing nothing." (James 1:2-4)

Going deeper still:

Where can you see God in the contradictions of life that surround you? How is God showing you His goodness, courage and comfort in the season that you are in?

Let's pray...

Lord, sometimes I feel so inadequate and unable. Sometimes I feel like I've lost more than I've gained. Please help me to know you as my light in the darkness, as my comfort in grief, and my provision in lack. Help me know you more, whether in good times or hard times. Amen.

DAY 20:
ALIEN INVASION

——·——

"Turn my eyes from worthless things, and give me life through
your word."
(Psalm 119:37)

Kingdom fruitfulness comes from drawing Kingdom nutrients
from the soil we're planted in. Remaining in Christ, rooted in the
Word of God and drawing truth into our core, enables our lives
to bear Kingdom fruit as a natural bi-product.

Yet just as a tree can suffer from external factors, so can we. A
healthy tree is not merely dependent on healthy roots for healthy
fruit. Its environment is also really important. Even a healthy
tree can be vulnerable to infestation from leaf-attacking, fruit-
invading, bark-biting parasites and fungi. Parasites gain their life
and energy by drawing the life out of – even injecting poison into
– a once healthy tree, with potentially fatal results.

Growing up I remember hearing of the fatal consequences
of Dutch Elm Disease making its way to Europe as the deadly
Ophiostoma novo-ulmi fungus spread by the tiny Elm Bark
Beetle destroyed many Elm trees. Hundreds of trees succumbed
to its ravages. In the USA, another tree disease called "Sudden
Oak Death" causes extensive damage to oaks and other trees,
beginning with the new shoots and then spreading to the whole
tree. When an alien infection seeps from leaf to branch to

trunk, it will eventually weaken the roots. Then death grips and overpowers it.

We should consider what parasites try to destroy us. In our roots and shoots, offence and un-forgiveness are like parasites to the great Oak, or like beetles to Elm trees. Attacks assault us from the outside – from our circumstances and environment – and can quickly penetrate our mind and hearts to the core. The battle is on. Can our roots draw deeper truth from the Word of God than our hearts can absorb hurt from offence?

In so many ways, offensive situations are inevitable. They are like fungal spores surrounding a tree. It's in the air. Unavoidable. Offence can latch on at any moment. We can take offence for what someone has, or hasn't, said or done. It can be personal or we can even get offended on behalf of someone else. How we respond to offence makes a huge difference. Offence can be nurtured and grown or nipped in the bud and removed.

Whilst we can't control the offence that others might take against us, we are responsible for guarding our own hearts against it. What happens when the parasite of offence lands on us and we are hurt, offended, or upset by something someone has done? The race is on. Will the impact of the hurt penetrate our heart quicker than truth drawn from the Word of God? If the hurt wins and becomes rooted, then our hearts will become susceptible to further wounds. Hardness and bitterness might spawn and bear fruit. Relational openness to the offender, or others, can quickly clog us up. We may change, become defensive and avoid connection. Perhaps the disease easily strangles our desire and ability to take Kingdom risks, hampering our obedience to Christ? The risk of being hurt again can seem too great. To protect our hearts then, we should consider again who we are rooted in.

The prophet Isaiah foretold the coming Servant, the Christ, saying,

"All of us, like sheep, have strayed away. We have left God's paths to follow our own. Yet the Lord laid on him the sins of us all. He was oppressed and treated harshly, yet he never said a word. He was led like a lamb to the slaughter. And as a sheep is silent before the shearers, he did not open his mouth. Unjustly condemned, he was led away. No one cared that he died without descendants, that his life was cut short in midstream. But he was struck down for the rebellion of my people. He had done no wrong and had never deceived anyone. But he was buried like a criminal; he was put in a rich man's grave." (Isaiah 53:6-9)

We look on in wonder at Christ, who did not take offence. As the writer of Hebrews said,

"Think of all the hostility he endured from sinful people; then you won't become weary and give up. After all, you have not yet given your lives in your struggle against sin." (Hebrews 12:3-4)

No accusation against you is ever going to surpass what Jesus endured for you.

Isaiah continues,

"But it was the Lord's good plan to crush him and cause him grief. Yet when his life is made an offering for sin, he will have many descendants. He will enjoy a long life, and the Lord's good plan will prosper in his hands. When he sees all that is accomplished by his anguish, he will be satisfied. And because of his experience, my righteous servant will make it possible for many to be counted righteous, for he will bear all their sins." (Isaiah 53:10-11)

Jesus saw beyond the voices of His accusers to the Lord's bigger plan. In the same way, as we remain rooted in Him, we too can live beyond the accusing voices – whether that comes from other people, or our spiritual enemy.

When Paul wrote to the Roman believers he wanted them to grasp the truth that Jesus knew them better than anyone else. He understood their hearts, their motivations, what they thought.

"And we know that God causes everything to work together for the good of those who love God and are called according to his purpose for them. For God knew his people in advance, and he chose them to become like his Son, so that his Son would be the firstborn among many brothers and sisters. And having chosen them, he called them to come to him. And having called them, he gave them right standing with himself. And having given them right standing, he gave them his glory." (Romans 8:28-30)

When offence threatens us, our first response should not be to try and defend ourselves, but to allow the Lord to defend us. We can depend on what God says is true about us, and draw on that truth, refusing to take offence. We can be confident that He knows us better than anyone, and if we remain in Him and love Him the most, He will work things out for the good – like He always has and always will. What a great truth to spur us on today!

Lies will surround us because the enemy *"prowls around like a roaring lion, looking for someone to devour"* (1 Peter 5:8). But, these lies are just enemy propaganda. They need not penetrate our hearts. Instead we can be rooted and *"stand firm against him, and be strong in (our) faith."*

Meditate on this:

"My child, pay attention to what I say. Listen carefully to my words. Don't lose sight of them. Let them penetrate deep into your heart, for they bring life to those who find them, and healing to their whole body. Guard your heart above all else, for it determines the course of your life." (Proverbs 4:20-23)

Going deeper still:

In what ways have you taken offence against others? Can you

prayerfully confess those things today? Take a moment to allow the Lord to soften your heart and bring healing and life back to you.

Let's pray...

Lord, I am sorry for the times when I've caused offence to anyone and hurt them, whether I was aware of it at the time or not. Please forgive me and allow that relationship to glorify you more. Father, where I have taken offence, I ask that you forgive me and help me to forgive those who have wronged me, that I might glorify you even more. Amen.

DAY 21:
SIGNIFICANT ROOTS FOR BIG FRUITS

———•———

"I pondered the direction of my life, and I turned to follow your laws."
(Psalm 119:59)

It's wonderful to see fully developed fruit that is mature and ripe, ready to pick and enjoy. But before we get to that stage, there is much secret root work that has to take place. It's the same with us – in due course our fruit will be visible, but the growth that leads to the fruit first takes place in the unseen places of our hearts.

When my children were little they often used to come back from their nursery or reception classes with various "treasures" they'd created or painted to share with us at home. Another activity popular in those days was growing cress seeds, and they would arrive home with a damp piece of cotton wool stuffed into an empty yoghurt pot, with a few little cress seeds scattered on top. The cress didn't seem bothered by the cotton "soil" and was happy to put its tiny roots down and its flimsy shoots up. Very quickly, impatient children were satisfied with a visible harvest from their little seeds. Sprouting over the top of the yogurt pot, the little cress stalks were snipped off and served in the only way possible – in an egg sandwich!

Cress is a wonderful plant for small children because it produces its "fruit" rapidly. The same cannot be said for the

Chinese Bamboo Tree. Like most plants, Bambusoideae needs to be nurtured and the seeds placed in fertile soil, with light and water to sustain them. But there won't be any signs of life for the first year after planting them – or the second year for that matter. In fact, there won't be any visible sign of growth for a whole five years! Nothing, zero, zip! No signs of life above the soil.

If it were possible to see beneath the soil, however, you would witness a huge amount of activity. Roots growing down deeper and deeper. Then, in the fifth year, something quite remarkable happens. It grows! Not just a little, peeking above the surface, but massive, fast, exponential growth. It can grow eighty feet within six weeks! Growth at that rate is almost visible to the human eye!

I was chatting with a friend recently who went on holiday for three weeks. The trousers she wore as she travelled out were set aside as the perfect travel-home item of clothing. However, after three weeks of "all inclusive" holiday making, these particular trousers could no longer get past the holiday hips!

When I was about fourteen years old my family went on a walking holiday in Austria. I remember it fondly as an excellent time. However, one of the stories that has been re-told many times (this might be the last time!) was that I had a growth spurt and grew two inches (upwards) in those two weeks. My trousers, which were full length at the start of the holiday, looked remarkably cropped by the end.

Growth can be visible sometimes. Sometimes it can be quick and present us with a trouser challenge! But our spiritual growth is characterised by a whole heap of hidden activity in the secret place. Spiritually, we grow much more like Chinese Bamboo trees – a great deal will happen inside of us, unseen, in order to be able to support the growth of what will, one day, be clearly visible. Like the bamboo, the strongest, biggest growth, requires the strongest, yet invisible roots to be in place. What has been grown in the secret place will determine what is sustainable in the visible place. As we consider the Sovereign Gardener's timing in our lives, it can be very challenging for us to appreciate the root work He needs to do in us, and to be patient through that process.

As David acknowledged in Psalm 139, the Lord works in the secret place preparing magnificent works to be revealed in His perfect time:

"You made all the delicate, inner parts of my body and knit me together in my mother's womb. Thank you for making me so wonderfully complex! Your workmanship is marvellous – how well I know it. You watched me as I was being formed in utter seclusion, as I was woven together in the dark of the womb. You saw me before I was born. Every day of my life was recorded in your book. Every moment was laid out before a single day had passed." (Psalm 139:13-16)

As we grow in our confidence of who the Father is for us, we can be certain that, even when we can't see things happening in our lives, He is at work in the unseen place. He works in the hiddenness. In His perfect time He will renew, restore, refresh and reveal us.

As Paul told the believers in Philippi, *"I am certain that God, who began the good work within you, will continue his work until it is finally finished on the day when Christ Jesus returns."* (Philippians 1:6)

As we continue to remain in Christ and learn to trust the Gardener, we can wait expectantly and confidently, knowing that His craftsmanship is excellent and everything He does is for our good and for His glory.

Meditate on this:

"'So – who is like me? Who holds a candle to me?' says The Holy. Look at the night skies: Who do you think made all this? Who marches this army of stars out each night, counts them off, and calls each by name – so magnificent! So powerful! – And never overlooks a single one? Why would you ever complain, O Jacob, or, whine, Israel, saying, 'God has lost track of me. He doesn't care what happens to me'? Don't you know anything? Haven't you been listening? God doesn't come and go. God lasts. He's Creator of all you can see or imagine. He doesn't get tired out, doesn't pause to catch his breath. And he knows everything, inside and out. He energises those who get tired, gives fresh strength to dropouts. For even young people tire and drop out, young folk in their prime stumble and fall. But those who wait upon God get fresh strength. They spread their wings and soar like eagles, they run and don't get tired, they walk and don't lag behind." (Isaiah 40:25-31 MSG)

Going deeper still:

What has the Lord begun in your life that is not yet completed? What do you think He is doing in the hidden place of your heart right now that requires you to wait confidently?

Let's pray…

Father, I thank you that even as you made me in the unseen place of my mother's womb, so you continue to work in the hidden places in my heart. Lord, I want you to complete what you have begun and I will trust you to bring the fruit into my life and through my life at the right time. Amen.

DAY 22:
WITH ADDED LOSS

———•———

"I weep with sorrow; encourage me by your word."
(Psalm 119:28)

There are some seasons in life when pruning can take on a whole new dimension. Seasons of loss and grief or bereavement can leave us feeling like our whole life has been drastically "chopped". Death, even in circumstances where it ends the suffering of a love one, never seems to come at the "right" time. There is never a "good" moment to lose someone; it is always an unwelcome intrusion. Yet even in our season of grief, the Father longs to meet with us and bring us His comfort.

Our earthly life is held in the tension of the "now-and-not-yet". Seeds of eternity are placed within each one of us. They will bear fruit in the future, in the "not-yet". Our lives on earth are really all root work for the fruit that will be borne eventually and carried into eternity. Earth is just the preparation for all that is to come. The writer of Ecclesiastes explains,

"God has made everything beautiful for its own time. He has planted eternity in the human heart, but even so, people cannot see the whole scope of God's work from beginning to end." (Ecclesiastes 3:11)

Recently I sat in a church service, not as a minister but as a bereaved friend. I joined to grieve with a friend who has lost his wife, the mother to their two young boys. Just a few days earlier I had sat with this friend and held her hand while she slept so deeply. It was a sleep she wouldn't wake from this side of Heaven. Our friendship had been precious, marked by many conversations about healing and eternal hope. She was on the edge of a healing miracle, but it wasn't one we were going to see this side of eternity. At her funeral I, like many others, struggled to unknot my voice and participate during the sung worship. I was really grateful to be standing next to someone with a confident voice who sang to make up for both of us. Tim was away, so there was no hand to hold and perhaps more than ever, I had to lean into the Father. During one of the songs, as my tears were falling, my eyes blurry, I saw something of the "now-and-not-yet" more clearly than I'd seen before. In that moment I knew the Holy Spirit was very close. The song was Lord, You Have My Heart. In this song there is a refrain where the women typically echo the men. We tried to oblige. As my grieving voice strained I heard the song differently than I had ever heard it before. At that moment, I heard the lines sung by the men as they normally sounded. But I heard the women's lines as if they were being sung by my friend, joining in with Heaven's choir. Suddenly, in my grief, I received a different understanding of the words.

(from earth) And I will praise you Lord
(from Heaven) I will praise you Lord
(from earth) And I will sing of love come down
(from Heaven) I will sing of love come down
(from earth) And as you show your face
(from Heaven) Show your face
(together) We'll see your glory here.

As I struggled to sing in praise on earth, I knew that my friend was exuberantly singing praises in Heaven. We were united in our song, worshipping from different sides of eternity. Me in weakness and she now in strength. She was suddenly in the "now", while I was still in the "not yet". Somehow in that moment, our worship separated only by the invisible doorway from the now to the not-yet. She was in the other room.

As Jesus told His disciples,

"Don't let your hearts be troubled. Trust in God, and trust also in me. There is more than enough room in my Father's home. If this were not so, would I have told you that I am going to prepare a place for you? When everything is ready, I will come and get you, so that you will always be with me where I am. And you know the way to where I am going." (John 14:1-4)

I once heard of a father who had lost his young son. He hated the increasing number of days that separated his "now" from the time the child had tragically died. He didn't want time to stretch so that the memories faded. But the distance was growing and with every passing day the sense of loss just intensified. Comfort came to that father one day when, through the tears, he saw hope. He came to realise that because of Christ alone, every day without his beloved son on earth was one day closer to their reunion in Heaven. Our grief is not without hope. Rather, grief has hope wrapped within it.

Paul knew what it was to grieve, but he also understood that when we're in Christ our grief is different from those not in Christ.

"And now, dear brothers and sisters, we want you to know what will happen to the believers who have died so you will not grieve like people who have no hope. For since we believe that Jesus died and was raised to life again, we also believe that when Jesus returns,

God will bring back with him the believers who have died." (1 Thessalonians 4:13-14)

We have already considered the promise that Jesus shared with the multitudes:

"God blesses those who mourn, for they will be comforted." (Matthew 5:4)

As Jesus hung between two criminals on the cross, moments away from His last breath, He was still bringing comfort and strength to someone who was also moving from the "now" into "forever". A brief exchange of words took place: *"One of the criminals hanging beside him scoffed, 'So you're the Messiah, are you? Prove it by saving yourself – and us, too, while you're at it!' But the other criminal protested, 'Don't you fear God even when you have been sentenced to die? We deserve to die for our crimes, but this man hasn't done anything wrong.' Then he said, 'Jesus, remember me when you come into your Kingdom.' And Jesus replied, 'I assure you, today you will be with me in paradise.'"* (Luke 23:39-43)

The emptiness of losing someone to death is only really comforted by finding the One who is even greater in life. In Jesus we find comfort in the assurance of the transition from the "now" to the "not-yet".

Meditate on this:
"For this is how God loved the world: He gave his one and only Son, so that everyone who believes in him will not perish but have eternal life." (John 3:16)

Going deeper still:
In what ways have you known the comfort of the Lord in seasons of loss and grief?

Let's pray...

Lord, when we look ahead, life often seems like it is unfolding slowly, yet when we look back, we realise how fast it has gone by. Help me live every day in such a way that I honour you, loving and valuing everyone around me. Thank you that because of you, Jesus, eternal life is assured. Thank you for the loved ones you've blessed my life with. Lord, help me to trust all of them to you. Amen.

DAY 23:
ASK AGAIN

——•——

"Listen to my prayer; rescue me as you promised."
(Psalm 119:170)

As we continue to get to know the Gardener, we begin to understand a little more about His timing –and if we are wise, this can help us when we carry unanswered prayers. There are times when it seems that the things we're praying for are not reaching who we're praying to. When it feels like our prayers are falling on closed ears, ignored or unaccepted. Unanswered prayers seem to emphasise our barrenness, our fruitlessness. How do we deal with the weariness of asking for things but seeing no results?

Remember the parable that Jesus told to His disciples to encourage them to persist in prayer:

"'There was a judge in a certain city,' he said, 'who neither feared God nor cared about people. A widow of that city came to him repeatedly, saying, "Give me justice in this dispute with my enemy." The judge ignored her for a while, but finally he said to himself, "I don't fear God or care about people, but this woman is driving me crazy. I'm going to see that she gets justice, because she is wearing me out with her constant requests!"' Then the Lord said, 'Learn a lesson from this unjust judge. Even he rendered a just decision in the end. So don't you think God will surely give justice to his chosen people who cry out to him day and night? Will he keep putting them

off? I tell you, he will grant justice to them quickly! But when the Son of Man returns, how many will he find on the earth who have faith?" (Luke 18:1-8)

God is not an unjust judge. He is our loving Father who, as Jesus says, will respond with justice to His chosen people, His children. Justice is being given fair treatment. It shows no prejudice, but rather affords equal dignity to all. Jesus encouraged His disciples to not give up, but to press on, to persevere; to be persistent in asking, expecting justice.

In addition, Jesus taught His disciples not to approach the Father with a "shopping list" of requests, but instead to seek His will, saying,

"Our Father in heaven, may your name be kept holy. May your Kingdom come soon. May your will be done on earth, as it is in heaven. Give us today the food we need." (Matthew 6:9-11)

Rushing to get our needs met is focusing on the what rather than the who. Jesus modelled and taught how to develop a passion for pursuing the Father's will above our own.

Remember when Jesus healed a man on the Sabbath and was questioned about it by those who sought to oppose Him? He responded saying,

"I tell you the truth, the Son can do nothing by himself. He does only what he sees the Father doing. Whatever the Father does, the Son also does. For the Father loves the Son and shows him everything he is doing." (John 5:19-20)

If Jesus only did what He saw His father doing, we should do the same. It follows that the Father desires us to pray prayers that line up with His will. Remaining in Christ will enable us to have His wisdom when it comes to the Father's will. We are not playing a guessing game, but rather discerning the will of God by the power of the Holy Spirit as we remain in Christ.

In Scripture, Hannah stands out as an example of how to deal with unanswered prayer (1 Samuel). It's the beautiful story of a young woman who knew exactly what it was to feel like her prayers were going unanswered and that she was being overlooked. Hannah lived in a time of history when the political system was chaotic. The rulers were corrupt, effectively absent.

Hannah was one of two wives of a man called Elkanah. Hannah could not bear children and her grief over her barrenness was compounded by the fact that wife number two, Peninnah, seemed able to bear children with ease. As the months passed and Hannah was unable to conceive, they turned into years marked by disappointment and heartbreak.

Gripped by grief, Hannah lost hope of having children and lost the motivation to embrace life. She appeared to simply go through the motions of living. She couldn't fully enter into the religious festivals with her husband and his extended family. She was inconsolable. Her husband loved her and he longed for him to be enough for her, but he wasn't. She was desperate for a child of her own. Then, one day the situation began to change.

Hannah was participating in a religious festival – a pilgrimage that was going to take her to a different place, in more ways than one. Rather than staying on the fringes, as had become her custom, Hannah was done with hiding her pain. She pressed forward to the entrance of the temple – close enough to be observed by Eli the priest. Recorded in Scripture for the first time, Hannah bowed before the Lord. Consumed by pain, broken hearted, completely vulnerable and without pretence, she cried out. She was at the end of herself. She couldn't keep up appearances any more.

Aware of her own inability, she recognised that the only provider of life was the Lord Himself. So on her knees she begged him for a son. Hannah's desire for a son appears not to be selfish

– she wanted to bear fruit. It wasn't just that she wanted a baby to hold and raise, to parade as her own. If it had been all about her, she wouldn't have prayed the Kingdom prayer that came out of her mouth:

"And she made this vow: 'O Lord of Heaven's Armies, if you will look upon my sorrow and answer my prayer and give me a son, then I will give him back to you. He will be yours for his entire lifetime, and as a sign that he has been dedicated to the Lord, his hair will never be cut.'" (1 Samuel 1:11)

She surrendered her maternal desires to the Lord. Even in her state of desperate brokenness, she submitted to the Father's will and aligned with His desires. Doing so enabled her fruitfulness to be dedicated to the Lord's glory and not her own. The Lord longs for people to be dedicated to Him, so why would He not agree to grant her request? Hannah's prayer was no longer about herself – what she wanted in life, the child she yearned for – it was about God's will being fulfilled through her. She literally dedicated the fruit of her womb to the Lord. What a challenge!

After putting the Kingdom of God first in her life, Hannah went on to have her desire for child raising satisfied. The Lord blessed her with further children as, *"The Lord gave Hannah three sons and two daughters. Meanwhile, Samuel grew up in the presence of the Lord"* (1 Samuel 2:21).

Mediate on this:

"Keep on asking, and you will receive what you ask for. Keep on seeking, and you will find. Keep on knocking, and the door will be opened to you. For everyone who asks, receives. Everyone who seeks, finds. And to everyone who knocks, the door will be opened. You parents – if your children ask for a loaf of bread, do you give them a stone instead? Or if they ask for a fish, do you give them a

snake? Of course not! So if you sinful people know how to give good gifts to your children, how much more will your heavenly Father give good gifts to those who ask him." (Matthew 7:7-11)

Going deeper still:

What are you asking God for, longing for? Can you dedicate what you are longing for to the Lord, trust Him with your request and then say, "Let your will be done"? Will you keep asking?

Let's pray...

Lord, I thank you for the many times that you have answered prayers. Thank you that you are listening. Lord, help me get to know you, my Father, the Gardener, so that my prayers will come in line with your will. Lord, let me know your will and may your will be done in my life, starting today. Amen.

DAY 24:
HIS FINGERPRINTS ARE OVER YOU

———•———

*"Your regulations remain true to this day, for everything serves
your plans."*
(Psalm 119:91)

Remaining in Christ and trusting the Gardener to do what He
does best presents an interesting question: is God sovereign over
everything in your life? Can you see His fingerprints all over your
life?

There is a lie that has penetrated our everyday speech – one
that I believe the Gardener wants to prune. It is the language of
"luck".

The words that make up our language originate from our hearts
and mind set. As Jesus taught,

*"The words you speak come from the heart – that's what defiles
you. For from the heart come evil thoughts, murder, adultery, all
sexual immorality, theft, lying, and slander. These are what defile
you. Eating with unwashed hands will never defile you."* (Matthew
15:18-20)

The lie of luck is one which robs God of His glory, prevents us
from giving thanks, and implies there are limits to His providence.
Our culture has embraced the concept of luck, chance, chaos and
randomness. "Lucky for some ... I've been lucky ... Lady luck..."
When things go well for someone, we say they've been lucky.

When we avoid an accident or a traffic jam we say, "Wow, that was lucky." People are quick to acknowledge luck, rather than giving thanks and credit to God.

But the truth is, God's providence peppers every page of the Word of God, because He is sovereign. Nothing happens by random chance because the Lord is continually outworking His sovereign plans and purposes.

Let's consider the story of Joseph in Genesis – the dreamer-boy who irritated his brothers so much due to the unmerited favouritism he received from their father. The brothers made the most of an opportunity and hatched a plan to kill him. But God had a plan for Joseph's life and it was divine providence that prompted Reuben to insist they put Joseph in a cistern and not immediately kill him. It was providence that brought the Midianite traders along who bought him as a slave. It was providence that Joseph ended up in Potiphar's household and we read that,

"The Lord was with Joseph, so he succeeded in everything he did as he served in the home of his Egyptian master. Potiphar noticed this and realised that the Lord was with Joseph, giving him success in everything he did. This pleased Potiphar, so he soon made Joseph his personal attendant. He put him in charge of his entire household and everything he owned." (Genesis 39:2-4)

Not long after, it was providence that enabled Joseph to go to the royal prison as a result of a false accusation where, despite his circumstances, God continued to reveal His sovereignty through his life:

"The Lord was with Joseph in the prison and showed him his faithful love. And the Lord made Joseph a favourite with the prison warden. Before long, the warden put Joseph in charge of all the other prisoners and over everything that happened in the prison. The warden had no more worries, because Joseph took care of

everything. *The Lord was with him and caused everything he did to succeed."* (Genesis 39:21-23)

It was the Lord's providence that enabled Joseph to meet Pharaoh's former cup-bearer in prison, who had a confusing dream (which Joseph could interpret), so that when the cup-bearer was back serving Pharaoh he remembered Joseph. It was providence that meant Pharaoh had a dream and needed Joseph to come and bring God's interpretation.

Furthermore, it was God's sovereign plan that Joseph would end up serving Pharaoh and become the most powerful man in Egypt during a time of famine. It meant that when Joseph's family came looking for supplies, God's providence had already put Joseph in a place to respond. Joseph didn't say, "It's lucky that I'm here for you...", he recognised the sovereign hand of God at work.

"God has sent me ahead of you to keep you and your families alive and to preserve many survivors. So it was God who sent me here, not you! And he is the one who made me an adviser to Pharaoh – the manager of his entire palace and the governor of all Egypt." (Genesis 45:7-8)

We can be very confident that as we remain in Christ, every detail of our lives will be watched over and cared for by our Father. As Paul said, *"Because we are united with Christ, we have received an inheritance from God, for he chose us in advance, and he makes everything work out according to his plan"* (Ephesians 1:11).

Trusting in the Gardener is to trust in His providence in our lives, that He will work everything out for us. He tends to each individual branch as well as the whole garden. As we remain in Christ, we recognise that the Lord is sovereign over all things:

"The Lord has made the heavens his throne; from there he rules over everything." (Psalm 103:19)

As Paul preached in Athens,

"He is the God who made the world and everything in it. Since he is Lord of heaven and earth, he doesn't live in man-made temples, and human hands can't serve his needs – for he has no needs. He himself gives life and breath to everything, and he satisfies every need. From one man he created all the nations throughout the whole earth. He decided beforehand when they should rise and fall, and he determined their boundaries. His purpose was for the nations to seek after God and perhaps feel their way toward him and find him – though he is not far from any one of us. For in him we live and move and exist." (Acts 17:24-28)

People around us might give credit to luck. But those rooted in Christ can, "Be thankful in all circumstances, for this is God's will for you who belong to Christ Jesus" (1 Thessalonians 5:18).

Meditate on this:

"He remembered us in our weakness. His faithful love endures forever. He saved us from our enemies. His faithful love endures forever. He gives food to every living thing. His faithful love endures forever. Give thanks to the God of heaven. His faithful love endures forever." (Psalm 136:23-26)

Going deeper still:

Remaining in Christ is to look to Him first and follow Him wholeheartedly. What are some of the things going on in your life that you can give thanks to God for? If you look back, there will be things that seemed almost insignificant at the time, but in fact were signs of God's providence, His fingerprints on your life.

Let's pray...

Lord, help me to recall the many blessings in my life that I can say thank you for today. Forgive me that I've received blessings and not always said thank you. I've taken them for granted or even put them down to luck. Thank you that everything that happens in my life can bring me closer to you and as I remain in Christ it will bring you pleasure. Amen.

DAY 25:
IN THE "HORRIBILIS"

———•———

"As I learn your righteous regulations, I will thank you by living as I should!"
(Psalm 119:7)

In 1992 Her Majesty the Queen of Great Britain gave a speech in which she famously said, "1992 is not a year on which I shall look back with undiluted pleasure. In the words of one of my more sympathetic correspondents, it has turned out to be an *annus horribilis*." For non-Latin readers, suffice to say she'd had a "horrible year"!

There are times when the things of life can seem to stack up against us. For us it might not be like the Queen's terrible year – with family scandals plastered across the tabloids, our Commonwealth realm being reduced, or one of our castles nearly burning down – but we can all experience testing seasons where it feels like the heat is on; years which are bruising and burdensome, as issue after issue needs to be dealt with. It may be challenges in relationships, physical, mental or emotional health, financial difficulties, employment challenges or other struggles. All we know is that the heat is on and we feel caught in a desert storm.

If, in our mind, our circumstances are the measuring stick for our fruitfulness, then we are in trouble. If, on the other hand, we are trusting in the Gardener, we know that He will take care of us and see us through even the toughest of seasons. Jeremiah reminds us that our fruitfulness is directly influenced by who we are depending on. If we are relying on ourselves, others, or anything that is a substitute for God Himself, then we will reap accordingly.

"This is what the Lord says: 'Cursed are those who put their trust in mere humans, who rely on human strength and turn their hearts away from the Lord. They are like stunted shrubs in the desert, with no hope for the future. They will live in the barren wilderness, in an uninhabited salty land. But blessed are those who trust in the Lord and have made the Lord their hope and confidence. They are like trees planted along a riverbank, with roots that reach deep into the water. Such trees are not bothered by the heat or worried by long months of drought. Their leaves stay green, and they never stop producing fruit. The human heart is the most deceitful of all things, and desperately wicked. Who really knows how bad it is? But I, the Lord, search all hearts and examine secret motives. I give all people their due rewards, according to what their actions deserve." (Jeremiah 17:5-10)

The stunted shrubs that Jeremiah speaks of are stuck in a permanent condition of immaturity, never reaching their full potential. Jesus taught His followers, *"unless you turn from your sins and become like little children, you will never get into the Kingdom of Heaven"* (Matthew 18:3). Jesus advocates a childlike trust. Being childlike is not the same as being "immature". In fact, it is vastly different. Jesus wasn't saying His disciples should remain in a permanent condition of immaturity, stunted in their growth. Rather He wanted them to live with humility and simplicity – simply trusting in their Father God for everything. Childlike followers of Christ can thrive, even in arid conditions.

They retain their potential and can still burst into life, unhindered by the dry seasons.

Our trust in God is rarely tested on sunny, walk-in-the-park days. It is the year-in-the-desert seasons that test where our trust is placed. James wrote,

"For you know that when your faith is tested, your endurance has a chance to grow. So let it grow, for when your endurance is fully developed, you will be perfect and complete, needing nothing." (James 1:3-4)

Acts records the story of Paul and Silas, who were en route to a prayer meeting when they came across a demonised young slave girl. Paul, in the authority of Christ, silenced the demons and cast them out. The girl found freedom from torment, but her boss wasn't too happy about it. It meant a loss of earnings for her slave master. A disagreement broke out in the town:

"A mob quickly formed against Paul and Silas, and the city officials ordered them stripped and beaten with wooden rods. They were severely beaten, and then they were thrown into prison. The jailer was ordered to make sure they didn't escape. So the jailer put them into the inner dungeon and clamped their feet in the stocks." (Acts 16:22-24)

Held in atrocious conditions, beaten and shackled in stocks, they surely had grounds for complaint! This surely qualifies as a desert experience. Yet as Luke continues the story we read that,

"Around midnight Paul and Silas were praying and singing hymns to God, and the other prisoners were listening. Suddenly, there was a massive earthquake, and the prison was shaken to its foundations. All the doors immediately flew open, and the chains of every prisoner fell off! The jailer woke up to see the prison doors wide open. He assumed the prisoners had escaped, so he drew his sword to kill himself. But Paul shouted to him, 'Stop! Don't kill

yourself! We are all here!' The jailer called for lights and ran to the dungeon and fell down trembling before Paul and Silas. Then he brought them out and asked, 'Sirs, what must I do to be saved?' They replied, 'Believe in the Lord Jesus and you will be saved, along with everyone in your household.' And they shared the word of the Lord with him and with all who lived in his household." (Acts 16:25-32)

At the darkest moment of the night, in their bleak circumstances, Paul and Silas were found praising God, worshipping Him in jail. Not limited by physical captivity or circumstances, they chose to worship the one who gave them ultimate freedom. They remained in Christ, rooted and drawing on His strength whilst seeking to bring Him glory.

Consider the fruit of their evening's worship: the jailer and his whole household were saved. They took the keys of true freedom into the jail with them and set the jailer free! They were fruitful even in the "desert" of prison.

Whatever the circumstances in our lives that can make us feel "locked up" or that we're having an *annus horribilis*, it is possible for us to hold fast, trust in God, and still bear fruit. Hold on, stay put, don't give up!

Meditate on this:

"For God has said, 'I will never fail you. I will never abandon you.'" (Hebrews 13:5)

Going deeper still:

Describe how you related to the Father when you were going through a horrible time in your life. In what ways were you able to worship Him during the hard times? How would you like to grow in this?

Let's pray...

Lord, I know that you are everywhere and there is nowhere I can go apart from you. Thank you that even in the heat you are enough for me. You are everything. You are my strength and my source of hope. Lord, help me remain rooted in you and bringing you glory. Amen.

DAY 26:
A-MAZING GROWTH

*"Your regulations remain true to this day, for everything serves
your plans."*
(Psalm 119:90)

My childhood home was very near one of the homes of Henry
VIII – Hampton Court Palace – and as unaccustomed as I am to
palatial living, I enjoyed the occasional visit. Those who've been
will know that one of its great features in the maze located in the
gardens – a series of pathways encased in tall hedges leading to
its hidden centre. The path to the centre is obscured by confusing
crossroad choices and dead ends.

Our faith journey can often feel a bit like a maze. Not so much
A-mazing, but rather frustratingly full of blocked pathways
and confusing crossroads. We desire to be fruitful, trusting the
Gardener to grow us and position us where He wants us – but
the route to our destination can seem tortuous and take much
longer than we'd like. What might the Father's purpose be in the
seemingly circuitous parts of our journey that take longer than
we would choose them to?

Let's revisit the story of Moses. When Pharaoh eventually set
the Israelites free from slavery and Moses led them towards the
Promised Land, that journey should have taken about eleven
days. Instead it took them forty years. Approximately fourteen

thousand, five hundred and eighty nine more days than officially necessary! Why? Was it their sin, slowness to learn, lack of faith and grumbling? Or was something else going on?

Perhaps the actual reason is one tinged with tragedy. Picking up the story in Exodus we read,

"When Pharaoh finally let the people go, God did not lead them along the main road that runs through Philistine territory, even though that was the shortest route to the Promised Land. God said, 'If the people are faced with a battle, they might change their minds and return to Egypt.' So God led them in a roundabout way through the wilderness toward the Red Sea. Thus the Israelites left Egypt like an army ready for battle." (Exodus 13:17-19)

Whilst there is some speculation about the meaning of the final sentence, there is an overall meaning that is clear: the Israelites looked like an army, but they were not an army!

A vast group of people marching towards freedom would have appeared quite threatening to others. Yet, these people were not trained, equipped, united and ready to follow battle commands. They were not the "real deal". They looked like something they weren't in reality. So the Lord protected them from a battle encounter and took them the long way round. Faced with a battle, the Israelites could have easily become overwhelmed, forgetting that their God was stronger than any enemy. So instead, God gave them time – as much as was necessary for them to understand the strength and power He wanted to make available for them. God was not in a rush with them. He's not in a rush with us, either.

God's timing for things is rarely the same as ours.

"For you, a thousand years are as a passing day, as brief as a few night hours." (Psalm 90:4)

Peter picked up on this when he wrote,

"But you must not forget this one thing, dear friends: A day is

like a thousand years to the Lord, and a thousand years is like a day. The Lord isn't really being slow about his promise, as some people think. No, he is being patient for your sake. He does not want anyone to be destroyed, but wants everyone to repent." (2 Peter 3:8-9)

When we are frustrated with how long it seems to be taking the Lord to answer us, rescue us, or favour us, we might pause to consider: maybe He is the one who is waiting for us?

The context of Peter's words was the return of Christ, but the principle can be applied more broadly. Peter understood that people were waiting for God because He was waiting for them. What then, is the right response to God in such situations? Peter continues,

"And so, dear friends, while you are waiting for these things to happen, make every effort to be found living peaceful lives that are pure and blameless in his sight." (2 Peter 3:14)

As we live in the tension of the "meanwhile", we are to live peaceful, pure and blameless lives, remaining rooted in Christ as we trust the Father to fulfil His promises. The Lord longs for our authenticity as we wait for Him. He longs for us to be the "real deal" – unlike the faux-army that was the Israelites leaving Egypt. Remember how Jesus rebuked the Pharisees for their religious pretence, referring to them as "whitewashed tombs" (Matthew 23:27)? It is the state of our hearts before God that really matters. Remember that it's not just us who wait for the Lord, but He also waits for us. Waits for us to understand the extent of His power and provision in our lives. Oh, that we might be found remaining in Christ when the Lord comes to fulfil His promises! The Lord desires us to be living in such a way that we are known to be His, living an authentic lifestyle.

Meditate on this:

"But as for you, be strong and courageous, for your work will be rewarded." (2 Chronicles 15:7)

Going deeper still:

In what ways have journeys with the Lord taken longer than you thought? As a result of the delay what have you learned about God?

Let's pray…

Father, I thank you that whilst we see time differently, I can continue to trust you as you wait for me. Lord, please help me to not give up, but to remain in you, that the fruit of salvation to others might be my reward. Amen.

Section 3

EXPECT MORE

"I am the true grapevine, and my Father is the gardener. He cuts off every branch of mine that doesn't produce fruit, and he prunes the branches that do bear fruit so they will produce even more ... Remain in me, and I will remain in you. For a branch cannot produce fruit if it is severed from the vine, and you cannot be fruitful unless you remain in me. Yes, I am the vine; you are the branches. Those who remain in me, and I in them, will produce much fruit. For apart from me you can do nothing ... When you produce much fruit, you are my true disciples. This brings great glory to my Father. I have loved you even as the Father has loved me. Remain in my love. When you obey my commandments, you remain in my love, just as I obey my Father's commandments and remain in his love. I have told you these things so that you will be filled with my joy. Yes, your joy will overflow! ... Now you are my friends, since I have told you everything the Father told me. You didn't choose me. I chose you. I appointed you to go and produce lasting fruit, so that the Father will give you whatever you ask for, using my name. This is my command: Love each other."

(John 15:1-17)

DAY 27:
SEASONS

———·———

"I rise early, before the sun is up; I cry out for help and put my
hope in your words."
(Psalm 119:147)

We're going to spend the next few days taking an even close look at the fruit of our lives that is produced when we remain in Christ and trust the Gardener to bring about that fruitfulness, for His glory. Remember the words of the Psalmist:

"But they delight in the law of the Lord, meditating on it day and night. They are like trees planted along the riverbank, bearing fruit each season. Their leaves never wither, and they prosper in all they do." (Psalm 1:2-3)

* * *

In the UK we love to talk about the weather! Whereas many countries have sunshine in the summer and snow in the winter, as one might expect, not so with the United Kingdom! But we still recognise the changing of the seasons and there is much we can learn from them. Seasons are important and are referred to throughout Scripture:

"...as long as the earth remains, there will be planting and harvest, cold and heat, summer and winter, day and night." (Genesis 8:22)

Seasons are a natural part of the way God works with us, and there is an identifiable rhythm to our fruitfulness as we transition through the different seasons. Usually, as we have already seen, a season of growth will have been preceded by a season of God working in the unseen places of our lives. As David noted,

"You watched me as I was being formed in utter seclusion, as I was woven together in the dark of the womb. You saw me before I was born. Every day of my life was recorded in your book. Every moment was laid out before a single day had passed." (Psalm 139:15-16)

We were formed in the hidden place of our mother's womb until the time appointed for us to emerge. In the same way, as we grow as disciples there are further seasons of hiddenness followed by visible fruitfulness. Remember the Chinese Bamboo Plant!

The writer of Ecclesiastes talked about the seasons of life:

"For everything there is a season, a time for every activity under heaven. A time to be born and a time to die. A time to plant and a time to harvest. A time to kill and a time to heal. A time to tear down and a time to build up. A time to cry and a time to laugh. A time to grieve and a time to dance. A time to scatter stones and a time to gather stones. A time to embrace and a time to turn away. A time to search and a time to quit searching. A time to keep and a time to throw away. A time to tear and a time to mend. A time to be quiet and a time to speak. A time to love and a time to hate. A time for war and a time for peace." (Ecclesiastes 3:1-8)

Paul recognised the maturing seasons in his life:

"When I was a child, I spoke and thought and reasoned as a child. But when I grew up, I put away childish things." (1 Corinthians 13:11)

Perhaps it is time we too put away some childish things?

In order to be fruitful in our lives, it's helpful to understand and accept what season we're currently in – even if we don't know how long it will last.

There have been too many occasions in my life when I have wasted opportunities to be fruitful in a particular season, because I've been craving the fruit of a season still ahead – or even one that's been and gone. I'm sure you are all far too mature for this, but I personally wasted too much time with I'll-be-happy-when prayers! For example,

"I'll be happy when I have a boyfriend."

"I'll be happy when my exams are finished."

"I'll be happy when I get really great exam results."

"I'll be happy when I have my own place to live."

"I'll be happy when I'm married/when I'm divorced"

"I'll be happy when I'm well."

"I'll be happy when I have children/when my kids leave home/ when my kids move back home."

"I'll be happy when I get a better job/when I can stop working."

"I'll be happy when I have more friends, less fat, more money, less stress…"

…and so on!

The problem with this attitude is that it limits the extent of our Kingdom fruitfulness. In interrupts the season we are in by sowing seeds of discontent, which in turn produce their own harvest. For example, the stubborn weeds of jealousy. We know that the Lord wants us to bear fruit in every season, so we need to be mindful of the season we're in and not miss His purposes for it. We will be more fruitful if we keep our eyes on the "Lord of our future" rather than "our future for the Lord".

Paul wrote prayerfully to the Colossians,

"So we have not stopped praying for you since we first heard about you. We ask God to give you complete knowledge of his will and to give you spiritual wisdom and understanding. Then the way you live will always honour and please the Lord, and your lives will

produce every kind of good fruit. All the while, you will grow as you learn to know God better and better." (Colossians 1:9-10)

In a few days we will be looking at how we can expect more fruit to come. But first we need to allow the Lord to "position" us in each season for His purpose and His glory. What do I mean by this? In the story of Esther, her cousin Mordecai challenged her to accept where she was positioned as the Lord's providence. He told Esther, *"Who knows if perhaps you were made queen for just such a time as this?"* (Esther 4:14b). Esther had been removed from all that was familiar to her and placed by God in a position of influence – suddenly finding herself the unexpected Queen of Persia. In that position she was able to help the entire Israelite community to be spared from execution. Talk about fruitful in the season where we are planted!

Meditate on this:
"But the godly will flourish like palm trees and grow strong like the cedars of Lebanon. For they are transplanted to the Lord's own house. They flourish in the courts of our God. Even in old age they will still produce fruit; they will remain vital and green. They will declare, 'The Lord is just! He is my rock! There is no evil in him!'" (Psalm 92:12-15)

Going deeper still:
What season do you consider yourself to be in now? Or what season are you transitioning from? In what ways can you grow more rooted in this season?

Let's pray...
Father, please help me to be rooted in Christ where I'm planted now, in order that I might be fruitful for your glory. I trust you to lead me into the next season at the right time. Amen.

DAY 28:
NO LIMITS

———•———

"Even perfection has its limits, but your commands have no limit."
(Psalm 119:96)

In Paul's letter to the Galatians he writes contrasting the fruit that comes from the kingdom of the world and of the Spirit. Recognising the tension that exists between the two he writes,

"So I say, let the Holy Spirit guide your lives. Then you won't be doing what your sinful nature craves. The sinful nature wants to do evil, which is just the opposite of what the Spirit wants. And the Spirit gives us desires that are the opposite of what the sinful nature desires. These two forces are constantly fighting each other, so you are not free to carry out your good intentions. But when you are directed by the Spirit, you are not under obligation to the Law of Moses. When you follow the desires of your sinful nature, the results are very clear: sexual immorality, impurity, lustful pleasures, idolatry, sorcery, hostility, quarrelling, jealousy, outbursts of anger, selfish ambition, dissension, division, envy, drunkenness, wild parties, and other sins like these. Let me tell you again, as I have before, that anyone living that sort of life will not inherit the Kingdom of God. But the Holy Spirit produces this kind of fruit in our lives: love, joy, peace, patience, kindness, goodness, faithfulness, gentleness, and self-control. There is no law against these things! Those who belong to Christ Jesus have nailed the passions and

desires of their sinful nature to his cross and crucified them there. Since we are living by the Spirit, let us follow the Spirit's leading in every part of our lives. Let us not become conceited, or provoke one another, or be jealous of one another." (Galatians 5:16-26)

We have already looked at how we are divinely designed to be fruitful "after our own kind". As we remain in Christ, we will produce fruit in our life after His own kind. If we live apart from Christ, then the fruit produced will not be His kind of fruit.

Notice that Paul says, when referring to the fruit of the Spirit, *"There is no law against these things!"* (Galatians 5:23). It's another way of saying that when the Holy Spirit is working in our lives, there are no limits, no boundaries, no point where "enough" has been reached. There is no limit to how much fruitfulness can be displayed through our lives, because there is no limit to the power and presence of Jesus, in whom we remain. Instead we can be filled to overflowing:

"I pray that God, the source of hope, will fill you completely with joy and peace because you trust in him. Then you will overflow with confident hope through the power of the Holy Spirit." (Romans 15:13)

Imagine your life with a limitless amount of love, joy, peace, patience, kindness, goodness, faithfulness, gentleness, and self-control.

Let's think about peace. Paul wrote of the limitless peace that is available in Christ saying,

"Don't worry about anything; instead, pray about everything. Tell God what you need, and thank him for all he has done. Then you will experience God's peace, which exceeds anything we can understand. His peace will guard your hearts and minds as you live in Christ Jesus." (Philippians 4:6-7)

We might feel that there is no limit to the things we have to worry about, but in fact, there is no limit to the peace available to us that far exceeds worry. God's peace wipes out anxiety and nervous thoughts. So many of us become gripped with worries and anxieties, as depressing or nervous thoughts overwhelm us. Yet, we have access to an abundant supply of peace that overflows through the Holy Spirit. We no longer have to live in a state of feeling overwhelmed. We can live in the truth of His overflowing peace.

Or imagine limitless love.

"Love never gives up, never loses faith, is always hopeful, and endures through every circumstance." (1 Corinthians 13:5)

No situation can exist where, if we are in Christ, we will ever run out of God's love. I've heard of couples in strained relationships say that they just don't love each other any more – they're out of love. Of course, it is possible to run out of human love, desire, interest and attraction. But if we are rooted in Christ's love, this is impossible! When our supply of love comes from Heaven, that supply will never fail. It will always endure because there is a limitless supply.

We can apply this to any situation: teenagers who feel like they don't love their exasperating parents; siblings who struggle to get along; work colleagues or neighbours who infuriate us. But when we feel like we can't love any more, we need to turn to Jesus and remain in Him. In Him there is a supernatural, abundant supply of love available. Don't be condemned, be encouraged! There are no limits because Jesus puts no limit on the resources, love and grace that He has for each of us.

On many occasions I've heard the fruit of the Spirit described like a fruit bowl: laden with variety, with each individual fruit having its own distinct flavour. I prefer to think of it like an orange: one fruit with individual segments. Each part can be appreciated on its own, but they are all part of a whole that fits together beautifully. They are all aspects of the same fruit. God's design for our fruitfulness is not so much a "pick-and-mix" selection, but rather a "have-it-all" proposition.

Over the next few days we're going to spend some time looking more closely at each of the "segments" that make up the fruit of the Spirit. We are going to explore the limitless abundance of Christ as we remain in Him.

Meditate on this:

"Think about the things of heaven, not the things of earth. For you died to this life, and your real life is hidden with Christ in God. And when Christ, who is your life, is revealed to the whole world, you will share in all his glory." (Colossians 3:2-4)

Going Deeper Still:

Consider the boundaries you have in your life. In what ways can you remove the limits you may be placing on God's supply through His Spirit and enter into a more limitless, overflowing expression of your life in the Holy Spirit?

Let's pray...

Lord, some of the limitations on my life have seemed so big – like the worries – but I thank you that you are never limited and you are my abundant Provider. Lord, help me to remain in you, rely upon you and live in the unlimited overflow of your Spirit. Amen.

DAY 29:
THE GREATEST OF THESE IS...

——•——

"Lord, give me your unfailing love, the salvation that you
promised me."
(Psalm 119:41)

John writes that the fruit of love will come from one root only:

"Anyone who does not love does not know God, for God is love."
(1 John 4:8)

To know God is to know love. Knowing the one who is Love enables love to bear fruit in our lives.

You might have heard the expression that we are "human beings, not human doings", encouraging us to shift our focus from what we do to who we are. There is wisdom in this, especially for the workaholic who needs to grow in their understanding that God doesn't love us for what we achieve.

When we have our "being" in Christ, we will become those who do His will – but being always comes before doing in God's Kingdom. This will be the fruit of remaining in Him. Jesus wants us to know how much our actions matter to Him. He said,

"Yes, just as you can identify a tree by its fruit, so you can identify people by their actions." (Matthew 7:20) and,

"When you produce much fruit, you are my true disciples. This brings great glory to my Father." (John 15:8)

God is love and so remaining in Him means that we will

produce fruit after His "own kind", which will lead to an abundance of love expressed through our lives. As Jesus said, we are to,

"Love each other. Just as I have loved you, you should love each other. Your love for one another will prove to the world that you are my disciples." (John 13:34-35)

Jesus also told His disciples,

"I have loved you even as the Father has loved me. Remain in my love. When you obey my commandments, you remain in my love, just as I obey my Father's commandments and remain in his love. I have told you these things so that you will be filled with my joy. Yes, your joy will overflow! This is my commandment: Love each other in the same way I have loved you. There is no greater love than to lay down one's life for one's friends. You are my friends if you do what I command. I no longer call you slaves, because a master doesn't confide in his slaves. Now you are my friends, since I have told you everything the Father told me. You didn't choose me. I chose you. I appointed you to go and produce lasting fruit, so that the Father will give you whatever you ask for, using my name. This is my command: Love each other." (John 15:9-17)

In the context of John's Gospel, Jesus was speaking to His disciples about their love for one another, but His love didn't stop there. Jesus' love had no limits and reached beyond borders to those who didn't know Him yet. Paul wrote,

"For we know how dearly God loves us, because he has given us the Holy Spirit to fill our hearts with his love. When we were utterly helpless, Christ came at just the right time and died for us sinners. Now, most people would not be willing to die for an upright person, though someone might perhaps be willing to die for a person who is especially good. But God showed his great love for us by sending Christ to die for us while we were still sinners. And

since we have been made right in God's sight by the blood of Christ, he will certainly save us from God's condemnation. For since our friendship with God was restored by the death of his Son while we were still his enemies, we will certainly be saved through the life of his Son. So now we can rejoice in our wonderful new relationship with God because our Lord Jesus Christ has made us friends of God." (Romans 5:5-11)

If we're honest, some people are easier to love than others! Consider the plethora of people in your world – your family, church, community, neighbours, work colleagues. And those beyond your immediate circle – politicians, leaders of other nations, people of other religions, people of other cultures etc. There will be those we naturally resonate with and those who rub us up the wrong way just by showing up! But if we are rooted in Christ, however we feel about others, loving them is not an optional extra of our faith (like an upgrade feature on a car that we can live without) – it's a non-negotiable requirement. Jesus loves all people and so must we, in His strength. We can't be selective.

Jesus has confided in us, revealing the heart and plan of the Father's love. As one "branch" to another, I want to encourage you to draw every particle of truth from Jesus' words: You are loved! You are chosen. You are appointed to be fruitful. All of the fruitfulness that comes from your life starts simply because you are loved.

To grow in love we first must grow in love! What do I mean? That in order to be one who can give love to others, we must first be in the habit of receiving God's love. The more of Christ that is in us, the more of Him will flow out of us. And He is love. Jesus wants to express His limitless love to others through us – therefore, we must not limit how much love He can pour into us. Reflecting on this further, John explains that,

"God showed how much he loved us by sending his one and only
Son into the world so that we might have eternal life through him.
This is real love – not that we loved God, but that he loved us and
sent his Son as a sacrifice to take away our sins. Dear friends, since
God loved us that much, we surely ought to love each other. No one
has ever seen God. But if we love each other, God lives in us, and his
love is brought to full expression in us." (1 John 4:9-12)

Our love for others is more fully expressed when we fully grasp
how loved we are. Love is the natural bi-product of the love we
have received and remain in.

Remember Jesus' response when He was quizzed on the law?

"'Teacher, which is the most important commandment in the
Law of Moses?' Jesus replied, 'You must love the Lord your God
with all your heart, all your soul, and all your mind. This is the first
and greatest commandment. A second is equally important: Love
your neighbour as yourself. The entire law and all the demands of
the prophets are based on these two commandments.'" (Matthew
22:36-40)

This is the big reveal: by loving the Lord wholeheartedly
we are rooting ourselves and remaining in Him. The second
commandment then becomes a promise of fruitfulness. In loving
the Lord we will love all people, like He does.

Love, is a fruit and is not to be kept in the secret place, but
rather revealed, demonstrated and given away.

Jesus loved us while we were still in our sin, when He didn't
agree with our behaviour or like what we were doing. Yet He
loved us. When we love as Christ loves, it will cross any barrier of
race, religion or gender.

Love is not the absence of difference, but rather a bridge across
diversity. Remember that we are designed to be distinct; not to
blend in, but to stand out. Love doesn't make us like everyone

else, it extends a bridge enabling us to reach anyone. Christ considered every person worth laying down His life for. We can do the same, in Him and through Him, and reach out in love to anyone because, *"Jesus Christ is the same yesterday, today, and forever"* (Hebrews 13:8).

Meditate on this:

"Love is patient and kind. Love is not jealous or boastful or proud or rude. It does not demand its own way. It is not irritable, and it keeps no record of being wronged. It does not rejoice about injustice but rejoices whenever the truth wins out. Love never gives up, never loses faith, is always hopeful, and endures through every circumstance." (1 Corinthians 13:4-7)

Going deeper still:

Read today's meditation verse again and instead of the word love, substitute your own name. Does it still read true? In what ways do you need to grow fruitful in love?

Let's pray...

Lord, help me today to receive fresh revelation of how much you love me and what you have done for me to show your love. Fill me afresh with your love that I might love others in the way that you do. Amen.

DAY 30:
REAL STRENGTH

———•———

"Joyful are those who obey his laws and search for him with all
their hearts."
(Psalm 119:2)

In our Western culture it has become acceptable for happiness to
be the number one goal of people's lives. People grow up with the
longing, "I just want to be happy", or wish it for their loved ones,
and this fuels their motivation for life.

It's not a new concept. In Ecclesiastes 3:12 Solomon, writing
about the futility of life from the viewpoint of the average person,
says,

"So I concluded there is nothing better than to be happy and
enjoy ourselves as long as we can."

The challenge with happiness, as the world defines it, however,
is that it is so often at the mercy of our circumstances and subject
to chance. People's happiness increases or decreases exponentially
depending on what is happening to or around them. A promotion
at work increases our happiness. But then exhaustion from
overwork reduces our happiness. Wellbeing increases it; sickness
reduces it. Happiness is an elusive, fickle thing.

Scripture speaks a lot about joy. Joy is not the same as happiness.
Happiness comes to us from outside, shaped by external factors.
Joy comes from within. The source of that joy is not our human

strength, it has a supernatural supply. It comes from being rooted in and remaining in Christ.

Rick Warren defines joy as, "the settled assurance that God is in control of all the details of my life, the quiet confidence that ultimately everything is going to be alright, and the determined choice to praise God in every situation."

Joy isn't affected by external circumstances or random events, because it comes from our inner rootedness and reliance on Christ. It means we can confidently declare,

"God causes everything to work together for the good of those who love God and are called according to his purpose for them." (Romans 8:28)

As we remain in Christ we can learn from His joy and,

"...we do this by keeping our eyes on Jesus, the champion who initiates and perfects our faith. Because of the joy awaiting him, he endured the cross, disregarding its shame. Now he is seated in the place of honour beside God's throne." (Hebrews 12:2)

Jesus chose the cross because He looked beyond it and saw joy. He looked right through the cross and saw the salvation of sinners. The pain of the cross was worth it to Him because He saw the restoration of children to their Heavenly Father. The joy set before the Lord was you and me restored into relationship with the Father. We are His joy!

Jesus looked beyond His circumstances, enduring all the accusations and suffering, because He saw us. This means that we can look beyond our circumstances and see Him! When we remain in Him we have hope. We have joy and we can say, like Horatio Spafford, "It is well with my soul." We can still be fruitful even in the heat of the desert; even during our *annus horribilis*.

John wrote about His joy being our joy, so that our joy will be mature and complete:

"I've loved you the way my Father has loved me. Make yourselves at home in my love. If you keep my commands, you'll remain intimately at home in my love. That's what I've done – kept my Father's commands and made myself at home in his love. I've told you these things for a purpose: that my joy might be your joy, and your joy wholly mature. This is my command: Love one another the way I loved you." (John 15:9-12 MSG)

Nehemiah took a career break from being cup-bearer to the king to respond to the cries of God's people from desolated Jerusalem. He realised that the city walls of Jerusalem needed to be repaired if the Israelites, returning from exile, had any chance of survival. God's people were at risk and he felt compelled to be part of the solution.

When the wall was completed and the Israelites were physically safe from enemy attacks, Nehemiah realised that the work was only half done. The wall might have been repaired, but the people were still "broken" – broken in their relationship to God. The broken wall was symbolic of their broken, compromised hearts that were no longer turned towards the Lord. So they re-gathered around the Word. They returned to truth. They dedicated themselves back to the Lord and re-rooted themselves through repentance and recommitment. Into this situation Nehemiah spoke of joy:

"Nehemiah continued, 'Go and celebrate with a feast of rich foods and sweet drinks, and share gifts of food with people who have nothing prepared. This is a sacred day before our Lord. Don't be dejected and sad, for the joy of the Lord is your strength!' And the Levites, too, quieted the people, telling them, 'Hush! Don't weep! For this is a sacred day.' So the people went away to eat and drink at a festive meal, to share gifts of food, and to celebrate with great joy because they had heard God's words and understood them." (Nehemiah 8:10-12)

The Lord's joy – of relationship restored – was the strength of the people and their joy came because they heard and understood the Word of God. In other words, they not only knew what the Word said but they did what it said. They became rooted in truth. Then their joy was complete because it came from the true source of joy – Himself.

Now, just as then, the Lord wants to repair communities, towns, cities and nations. He wants to bring about transformation and cause communities to thrive. However, His even greater longing is for our relationship with Him to be restored. His joy is relationship with us, and His joy will be our strength. Our joy will be complete when we remain, rooted, wholeheartedly obedient and committed to Him.

Meditate on this:
"I pray that God, the source of hope, will fill you completely with joy and peace because you trust in him. Then you will overflow with confident hope through the power of the Holy Spirit." (Romans 15:13)

Going Deeper still:
What circumstances have you allowed to determine your happiness? Looking beyond your circumstances to Christ Himself, what truth does He speak to draw you closer to Him?

Let's pray...
Lord, may you fill me with your joy and peace and help me trust you wholeheartedly. Today, may I see beyond my circumstances to where you are and know you more. Amen.

DAY 31:
PEACE

"Your promises have been thoroughly tested; that is why I love them so much."
(Psalm 119:140)

If a story makes it into three of the Gospels we can be sure that there is something important in it the Lord wants us to know about. So the story of Jesus' calming the storm at sea is one not to miss. Jesus and His disciples have come away from a crowded hilltop and are making a boat trip across the Sea of Galilee. Jesus, tired from ministry, has fallen asleep in the back of the boat. However, as was typical of the Sea of Galilee, the weather had turned quickly and a storm erupted.

The Gospel writers don't tell which disciples were in the boat at this time, but even if it wasn't all of them, it is most likely that some of the former fishermen are part of the team. As professional fishermen, they would have made numerous boat journeys and no doubt experienced some serious squalls over the years, but here they are recorded as being "terrified" as *"high waves were breaking into the boat, and it began to fill with water"* (Mark 4: 36). It must have been a very harsh storm. The heavy rain invaded their boat and the strong winds threatened to capsize it. They felt very unsafe!

It is one thing to be in difficult times with a storm raging around us. But, it is completely different when that storm is invading our space; when we're not just observing it, but experiencing it. This was not a storm they could see taking place in the distance, they were in it. They were experiencing the knots in their stomachs tightening, their fear growing, panic rising. The disciples were becoming drenched and desperate.

Notice that despite the fierce storm raging around them, Jesus was still resting peacefully. In fact, He didn't seem to notice it at all until he was woken up by His fear-filled-followers. In Mark and Luke's gospel, Jesus is shown to first quieten the noise of the surrounding storm and then He challenges the disciples' fear. Matthew brings a different emphasis. He records that,

"Jesus responded, 'Why are you afraid? You have so little faith!' Then he got up and rebuked the wind and waves, and suddenly there was a great calm." (Matthew 8:26)

Jesus was going to bring order to the "outer storm", but He was more concerned with addressing the disciples "inner storm" before that. The same is true for you and me: Jesus is more concerned with the condition of our heart than He is our circumstances.

Where was their faith? Couldn't one of them take their tiny, mustard seed sized faith and encourage the others that because Jesus was with them they had nothing to fear? Could none of these fishermen draw on their experience of what they'd seen Him do on other occasions, so surely this would be OK? Could they not allow the peace of God to rise quicker than the water? It seems that while Jesus was travelling with them, He was not yet travelling within them.

Later Jesus explained to His disciples that peace was something they could experience all the time saying,

"I am telling you these things now while I am still with you. But when the Father sends the Advocate as my representative – that is,

the Holy Spirit – he will teach you everything and will remind you of everything I have told you. I am leaving you with a gift – peace of mind and heart. And the peace I give is a gift the world cannot give. So don't be troubled or afraid." (John 14:25-27)

The Holy Spirit's presence with us is the gift of the presence of peace in our hearts and minds. It is the peace that comes from intimacy with the Spirit and leads to fullness of life. As Paul wrote,

"Don't worry about anything; instead, pray about everything. Tell God what you need, and thank him for all he has done. Then you will experience God's peace, which exceeds anything we can understand. His peace will guard your hearts and minds as you live in Christ Jesus." (Philippians 4:6-7)

When we face the storms of life, we can ask Jesus for help, but it's also good to remember what He has done before. When we recall what He has already done for us, we will be encouraged about what He will yet do for us, and we will grow more confident in His unchanging, consistent love. All too often our present situation can overshadow our previous experience.

When the boat finally stabilised and the storm subsided, the terrified disciples' response was to question, "'Who is this man?' they asked each other. 'Even the wind and waves obey him!'" (Mark 4:41). The truth was dawning on them that Jesus' power was even bigger than the storm. Peace came to the disciples as they realised again that nothing could overpower Jesus. The same is true for us and any storms we might face, whether external or internal. Jesus is more powerful and His peace is enough.

Although the disciples panicked as the storm hit the lake, they did one wise thing – they appealed to the Prince of Peace (Isaiah 9:6). Jesus is Peace personified, so as we remain in Him the fruit we will produce is His peace. We can experience the fruit of peace even when our circumstances suggest we should be experiencing anything but peace! Peace can reign, even in the midst of the storm. Peace comes from being rooted in the truth and filled with the Holy Spirit, so that despite the storm, we don't panic. Jesus can calm any storm. If a storm is raging in your life and Jesus still appears to be taking a nap, take courage. Call and ask Him to calm the storm. While you are waiting you can be confident that He has heard you, and you can still be at peace while you wait, knowing that everything is in His hands.

Remaining in Christ enables His peace to remain in us, and to reach others through us. The beautiful Hebrew word for peace, shalom, encapsulates both its wholeness and tranquillity, as well as its harmony. It describes the peace that has come between us and Father God, but also with each other. Shalom is within us and between us.

Meditate on this:

"I look up to the mountains – does my help come from there? My help comes from the Lord, who made heaven and earth! He will not let you stumble; the one who watches over you will not slumber. Indeed, he who watches over Israel never slumbers or sleeps. The Lord himself watches over you! The Lord stands beside you as your protective shade. The sun will not harm you by day, nor the moon at night. The Lord keeps you from all harm and watches over your life. The Lord keeps watch over you as you come and go, both now and forever." (Psalm 121:1-8)

Going deeper still:

Consider your storms, past and present. In what way could any of your storms be experienced differently if you grew in awareness of the presence of the Lord being with you and in you?

Let's Pray...

Lord, in the storms of my life that have been and gone I thank you for your presence, your protection, and your gift of peace that has grown. In the storms that are happening now, and in the ones that will come, Lord, may you fill me with your Holy Spirit that I will allow your peace to be more real to me than any storm I might face. May your peace be a fruit that is evident in my life and one that I experience daily. Amen.

DAY 32:
ALTITUDE, ATTITUDE AND APTITUDE

————•————

"Reassure me of your promise, made to those who fear you."
(Psalm 119:38)

"Thank you for your patience. Your call is important to us. We will be with you shortly," said the cheery voice in my ear. After the fifth time of hearing this I no longer felt very patient. I didn't feel that the company I was calling had the same interpretation of "shortly" as me. In fact, I no longer felt that my call was important to anyone on the planet, let alone the person I'd eventually, hopefully, get to speak to. I put my phone on hands-free and got on with some other things whilst I waited for my call to be dealt with, which helped soothe my frustration a little.

It's tempting to view patience as a passive activity. "Well, I'm waiting, so I can't do anything…" But in fact, it is an active choice. Like my multi-tasking with my phone on hands-free, we have a choice about what we do in the "meantime" moments, whilst we are waiting for God to answer our prayers.

Patience can be defined as "the capacity to accept or tolerate delay, problems, or suffering without becoming annoyed or anxious". Today we will consider three simple thoughts which will help us grow fruitful in patience: our altitude, our attitude and our aptitude.

Altitude is the height of an object in relation to the ground.

When we "can't see the wood for the trees" it helps to step back; to go to higher ground, so that we can take in the whole scene and see the bigger picture. Our "altitude" will significantly impact our perspective of any situation as we begin to see it as Jesus sees it. Remember the fruit of patience comes through us when Christ is within us – and He is the one who has the best perspective!

"'I am the Alpha and the Omega – the beginning and the end,' says the Lord God. 'I am the one who is, who always was, and who is still to come – the Almighty One.'" (Revelation 1:8)

"Only I can tell you the future before it even happens. Everything I plan will come to pass, for I do whatever I wish. I will call a swift bird of prey from the east – a leader from a distant land to come and do my bidding. I have said what I would do, and I will do it." (Isaiah 46:10-11)

While our perspective will always be limited, we can see that the Lord's is not. He sees all things. What He says will come to pass will come to pass. Our patience will grow when we seek the higher ground of God's presence. As we align ourselves with Him, we will begin to see things through His eyes.

How we wait is very significant. Our attitude is the way in which we think/feel about something.

James talks about the need for believers to be patient for the Lord to return, just like a farmer waits for rain.

"Dear brothers and sisters, be patient as you wait for the Lord's return. Consider the farmers who patiently wait for the rains in the fall and in the spring. They eagerly look for the valuable harvest to ripen. You, too, must be patient. Take courage, for the coming of the Lord is near. Don't grumble about each other, brothers and sisters, or you will be judged. For look – the Judge is standing at the door! For examples of patience in suffering, dear brothers and sisters, look at the prophets who spoke in the name of the Lord. We give

great honour to those who endure under suffering. For instance, you know about Job, a man of great endurance. You can see how the Lord was kind to him at the end, for the Lord is full of tenderness and mercy." (James 5:7-11)

Attitude is important. While we are waiting for the promised "rain" we are not to take our eyes off the harvest, knowing that it will come to fruition in God's time. Rather than staring at the clouds we keep our eyes focused on a vision of the harvest, with an attitude of faith, and without grumbling.

Finally, our *aptitude* – our "natural ability to do something". In a season that requires patience, most of us will vacillate between helpless frustration and trying to do something to fix our situation. Our aptitude can be a challenge. If we admit we are unable to do anything, then we have no choice but to wait. But if we are capable, able to do certain things for ourselves, then it can be tempting to try to "make something happen" – especially if we are naturally task orientated people.

We need wisdom. Remember that it's not just us who are waiting for the Lord, but sometimes He is waiting for us. Sometimes we need to be an active part of the solution, while at other times we just need to "rest" and focus on other things.

Abraham was told by the Lord to, *"Look up into the sky and count the stars if you can. That's how many descendants you will have!"* (Genesis 15:5). Abraham was already quite old when he was told this, and on a clear night he would have seen a lot of stars! That's a lot of descendants.

But despite the promise, their circumstances looked bleak. If you're going to have many descendants, you've surely got to have at least one natural born child to begin with, but Abraham and Sarah had none. They'd done what was necessary to conceive and it wasn't happening!

With the clock ticking, they tried to solve the situation themselves. Frustrated Sarah decided to take matters into her own hands and persuaded Abraham to be intimate with her servant and bear a child that way. The first "star" was born. Unfortunately, this was not the scenario the Lord intended and it spawned a number of problems. Eventually the promised child came, but not before Abraham and Sarah had created a whole lot of difficulties for themselves.

In waiting, Father God desires that patient obedience will grow in us, not that we will try to fix our problems on our own. It is humbling to have the aptitude to be able to do something, and to lay that down and say, "No, I will wait for the Lord." We become the most fruitful in patience when we depend on Him; when we trust in Him and refuse to take matters into our own hands. Instead, we look to the Lord to fulfil what He has promised.

In around 1934 American theologian Reinhold Niebuhr wrote a prayer, which has in more recent years been adopted by Alcoholics Anonymous and other Twelve Step programmes. The Serendipity Prayer speaks to our altitude, attitude and aptitude: "God, grant me the serenity to accept the things I cannot change, courage to change the things I can, and wisdom to know the difference."

Meditate on this:
"Yet I am confident I will see the Lord's goodness while I am here in the land of the living. Wait patiently for the Lord. Be brave and courageous. Yes, wait patiently for the Lord." (Psalm 27:13-14)

Going Deeper still:
Today, are you still waiting for something God has promised you?

If yes, how has He confirmed this to you? What does the Lord want to show you in these "meantime" moments?

Let's pray...
Lord Jesus, please help me to wait in you. Help me to trust you for your timing in my life, and in your will and desire for me. May I do what you want me to do and not anything else. Amen.

DAY 33:
A.R.K.

"Your promise revives me; it comforts me in all my troubles."
(Psalm 119:50)

One day, my eldest daughter was walking home from school when she came across a distressed mother coming towards her with a young, crying child in a pushchair. My daughter was nearly home when the woman stopped her to ask her for directions to the nearest hospital. Her child was very sick and the mother had decided that while an ambulance wasn't needed, the hospital was. My daughter started to give her directions but, realising the distressed lady was just getting confused, she decided to "become" the directions and escort the lady to the hospital herself; a walk of a few miles; a walk of kindness.

Kindness is the quality of being friendly, generous and considerate. Kindness is giving, not because you will get anything, but because you have something. In my daughter's case, she had the knowledge of the hospital's location and she gave that, along with her time. Kindness requires a soft-hearted approach even in hard situations.

Paul wrote to Titus reminding him of the unmerited favour and kindness he had received:

"But – when God our Saviour revealed his kindness and love, he saved us, not because of the righteous things we had done, but

161

because of his mercy. He washed away our sins, giving us a new birth and new life through the Holy Spirit. He generously poured out the Spirit upon us through Jesus Christ our Saviour. Because of his grace he made us right in his sight and gave us confidence that we will inherit eternal life. This is a trustworthy saying, and I want you to insist on these teachings so that all who trust in God will devote themselves to doing good. These teachings are good and beneficial for everyone." (Titus 3:4-8)

The Lord was kind because he had something we needed, namely mercy. The kindness of Jesus was not about what He could get, but because of what He could give.

In the fun Hollywood film Evan Almighty, Morgan Freeman plays the role of God alongside Steve Carrell's Noah. Naturally, God tells Noah to build an Ark, which he sets about doing in the heart of suburban America. One of the comic moments is when God spells out the word ARK to mean "Acts of Random Kindness" and encourages Noah to change his world. He tells him to be on the lookout to share random, generous, un-returnable kindnesses.

We too can learn how to grow in the fruit of kindness. Acts of Random Kindness are a way of generously giving to and blessing others – not because of what we can get, but because of what, or rather who, we can give. Out of the fullness of kindness and mercy that Jesus has poured into us, we can show kindness to those around us, and in so doing, show them Jesus. It doesn't have to be difficult: speaking a gentle word, opening a door, making a drink, giving way to another driver, smiling at a passer-by, welcoming a stranger, offering your seat on the train, being gracious to stressed shop assistants. We can easily find ways to be kind, expecting nothing in return. Is this fruit evident in our lives?

One day, when Jesus was at the Temple, a crowd gathered. A woman who had been caught in the act of adultery was dragged before Him. The Pharisees sought ways to trick Jesus into a self-condemning response. It was a trap and Jesus knew it. Instead, He drew a line in the sand, which took everyone's attention away from the woman and put it on Him. Standing He said,

"'...Let the one who has never sinned throw the first stone!' Then he stooped down again and wrote in the dust. When the accusers heard this, they slipped away one by one, beginning with the oldest, until only Jesus was left in the middle of the crowd with the woman. Then Jesus stood up again and said to the woman, 'Where are your accusers? Didn't even one of them condemn you?' 'No, Lord,' she said. And Jesus said, 'Neither do I. Go and sin no more.'" (John 8:7-11)

Jesus did not condemn her, rather He showed her kindness. He extended His mercy to cover her shame with dignity. He clothed her with kindness because He is kindness.

At the first bite of the forbidden fruit, when Adam and Eve chose to disobey God, we read that,

"At that moment their eyes were opened, and they suddenly felt shame at their nakedness. So they sewed fig leaves together to cover themselves." (Genesis 3:7)

Gripped by the impact of their own sin, they tried to cover up their shame. However, rather than allowing their sin to simply be covered up, our loving Father chose to clothe them with dignity as,

"The Lord God made garments of skin for Adam and his wife and clothed them." (Genesis 3:21)

Our response is to cover our sin, but the Lord's kindness means that He longs to clothe us with dignity. When we are filled with God's kindness, and understand how much He has forgiven us, that kindness spills over to touch others. We wear that kindness like a new set of clothes. As Paul wrote,

"Since God chose you to be the holy people he loves, you must clothe yourselves with tender-hearted mercy, kindness, humility, gentleness, and patience. Make allowance for each other's faults, and forgive anyone who offends you. Remember, the Lord forgave you, so you must forgive others. Above all, clothe yourselves with love, which binds us all together in perfect harmony. And let the peace that comes from Christ rule in your hearts. For as members of one body you are called to live in peace. And always be thankful." (Colossians 3:12-15)

As we remain in Christ we are rooted into kindness, drawing on all that He is to show to others. We can put on kindness because we are saved through His kindness.

Paul wrote to the Ephesians revealing God's mysterious master plan of salvation – His ultimate kindness to us – which enables us to enter into the purposes and fruitfulness He has for us:

"But God is so rich in mercy, and he loved us so much, that even though we were dead because of our sins, he gave us life when he raised Christ from the dead. (It is only by God's grace that you have been saved!) For he raised us from the dead along with Christ and seated us with him in the heavenly realms because we are united with Christ Jesus. So God can point to us in all future ages as examples of the incredible wealth of his grace and kindness toward us, as shown in all he has done for us who are united with Christ Jesus. God saved you by his grace when you believed. And you can't take credit for this; it is a gift from God. Salvation is not a reward for the good things we have done, so none of us can boast about it. For we are God's masterpiece. He has created us anew in Christ Jesus, so we can do the good things he planned for us long ago." (Ephesians 2:4-10)

A.R.K.

Meditate on this:

"Get rid of all bitterness, rage, anger, harsh words, and slander, as well as all types of evil behaviour. Instead, be kind to each other, tender-hearted, forgiving one another, just as God through Christ has forgiven you." (Ephesians 4:31-32)

Going deeper still:

Today, is there anyone you could be kinder to in regards to forgiving them, or showing un-returnable generosity towards them? Plan to do one significant Act of Random Kindness today.

Let's pray...

Jesus, I thank you that you have been and always will be kind towards me. Thank you that you have given me so much unmerited favour. Today, Lord, will you help me to see and make opportunities to do acts of random kindness for others. May I be gracious, kind and forgiving to all those I meet. Amen.

DAY 34:
PURSUED

———•———

"How sweet your words taste to me; they are sweeter than honey."
(Psalm 119:103)

David, the shepherd-boy-turned-king, gained many of his valuable lessons out in the fields, then took them with him into the palace courts and onto battlefields. He first knew friendship with the Lord as a shepherd boy, whether it was in the quiet, contemplative times, or when predators attacked. He went from killing lions and bears to thousands of enemy soldiers.

In possibly the best known psalm, David drew on all of his experiences as a shepherd to understand his relationship with the Lord and, in particular, his certainty of the Lord's goodness. David shows what it is to pursue and remain in the Lord in such a way that the Lord is shown both in him and through him.

"The Lord is my shepherd;
I have all that I need.
He lets me rest in green meadows;
He leads me beside peaceful streams.
He renews my strength.
He guides me along right paths,
bringing honour to his name.
Even when I walk
through the darkest valley,

I will not be afraid,
for you are close beside me.
Your rod and your staff
protect and comfort me.
You prepare a feast for me
in the presence of my enemies.
You honour me by anointing my head with oil.
My cup overflows with blessings.
Surely your goodness and unfailing love will pursue me
all the days of my life,
and I will live in the house of the Lord
forever." (Psalm 23)

David acknowledges that not only were all of his needs met by the Lord, His provider, but he was led, renewed, guided, walked with, protected by, comforted by, and honoured by the Lord. Remaining in the Lord meant that goodness and love pulsated through his life. Pursuing the Lord meant that David experienced the Lord's goodness pursuing him. For as long as David walked with the Lord, it was the Lord who was glorified.

When you pursue goodness, goodness will pursue you, because goodness follows obedience. That which you pursue will be what pursues you. Even as you remain in Christ, it is He who will be revealed through you.

Jesus taught His disciples about the importance of having our priorities right:

"Wherever your treasure is, there the desires of your heart will also be. Your eye is like a lamp that provides light for your body. When your eye is healthy, your whole body is filled with light. But when your eye is unhealthy, your whole body is filled with darkness. And if the light you think you have is actually darkness, how deep that darkness is!" (Matthew 6:21-23)

What a disciple pursues will impact what is shown through

his/her life.

Have you ever become so tired of doing something (even a good thing) that you simply can't be bothered to keep doing it anymore? I am sure you have! It can range from the trivial – loading the dishwasher, putting out the bins – to the important: always making an effort to speak the truth with kindness, or being the one who takes the initiative to nurture a relationship. Sometimes we just get weary of doing that thing and want to quit, don't we? Well, what if that something is goodness? Be honest, don't you sometimes get tired of doing good?

The believers in Galatia knew this feeling. So Paul, inspired by the life of Christ, encouraged them:

"Don't be misled – you cannot mock the justice of God. You will always harvest what you plant. Those who live only to satisfy their own sinful nature will harvest decay and death from that sinful nature. But those who live to please the Spirit will harvest everlasting life from the Spirit. So let's not get tired of doing what is good. At just the right time we will reap a harvest of blessing if we don't give up. Therefore, whenever we have the opportunity, we should do good to everyone – especially to those in the family of faith." (Galatians 6:7-10)

The reason it's hard to keep doing good – and why we need to be reminded – is simply due to the human condition and our propensity towards selfishness. As we read in Genesis,

"The Lord observed the extent of human wickedness on the earth, and he saw that everything they thought or imagined was consistently and totally evil. So the Lord was sorry he had ever made them and put them on the earth. It broke his heart." (Genesis 6:5-6)

Left to its own devices, human nature will always veer off course – like a car with worn out bearings that constantly wants to pull in another direction; effort is needed to compensate to steer in a straight line. Like a car that needs its steering fixing, God doesn't want us to pretend that we can steer our lives in a straight line – He wants to fix us, so that we can be guided by goodness and follow the path of His will.

Authenticity is the key principle when it comes to the fruit of goodness. Plenty of people try to be and do good. But, it is only when we are firmly rooted in Christ – He that is good – that we can bear this Kingdom fruit. As Paul said,

"Don't just pretend to love others. Really love them. Hate what is wrong. Hold tightly to what is good. Love each other with genuine affection, and take delight in honouring each other." (Romans 12:9-10)

The Lord has good plans ahead for us and good works to do through us. As it is written,

"'For I know the plans I have for you,' says the Lord. 'They are plans for good and not for disaster, to give you a future and a hope.'" (Jeremiah 29:11)

Remember too that,

"...we are God's masterpiece. He has created us anew in Christ Jesus, so we can do the good things he planned for us long ago." (Ephesians 2:10)

Without the life-source of the Holy Spirit filling us, we will eventually swerve off course. The less we are filled, the more the fruit of our selfishness will surface. The more we are filled, the more Kingdom fruit will be displayed. It is the Lord's desire that His good purposes come to pass in your life, now and in the days to come. For that to happen you must stay firmly rooted into Jesus. You, the branch, must stay connected to Him, the vine.

Meditate on this:

"Don't let evil conquer you, but conquer evil by doing good." (Romans 12:21)

Going deeper still:

How can you pursue the Lord's goodness more, in both "dark valleys" and "green meadows" alike?

Let's pray...

Lord, I thank you that your plans for me are good. I thank you that you promise to be found by me when I pursue you wholeheartedly and that your goodness will then pursue me. Lord, today may I be increasingly aware of your goodness in all the situations I face. Amen.

DAY 35:
FOREVER AND EVER

———•———

"In your faithful love, O Lord, hear my cry; let me be revived by following your regulations."
(Psalm 119:149)

Faithfulness is an expression of the fruit of the Spirit which will grow evident in our lives when we remain in Christ because it is fruit "after His kind". We can be faithful because He first is faithful. Looking back over time we can remind ourselves of who was, is, and always will be, the truest and most faithful one.

"Understand, therefore, that the Lord your God is indeed God. He is the faithful God who keeps his covenant for a thousand generations and lavishes his unfailing love on those who love him and obey his commands." (Deuteronomy 7:9)

Generation after generation the Lord has been faithful. Consider the story of Abraham. Ageing alongside his wife Sarah, the couple remained childless even though the Lord had made a covenantal promise guaranteeing countless descendants.

"I will make you extremely fruitful. Your descendants will become many nations, and kings will be among them!" (Genesis 17:6)

Approximately fifteen years after the first promise the Lord reminded Abraham in regard to Sarah,

"I will bless her and give you a son from her! Yes, I will bless her

richly, and she will become the mother of many nations. Kings of nations will be among her descendants." (Genesis 17:16)

Eventually Abraham and Sarah saw God's faithful fulfilment of His promise with the birth of Isaac. But remember what happened! Not many years had passed, and while Isaac was still a boy, the Lord said to Abraham,

"Take your son, your only son – yes, Isaac, whom you love so much – and go to the land of Moriah. Go and sacrifice him as a burnt offering on one of the mountains, which I will show you." (Genesis 22:2)

What a test! No doubt this story is familiar to you and you know the outcome (spoiler alert: ram caught in thicket!). But, we mustn't miss the message of the test too quickly. Would Abraham love the fruit of the promise more than he loved the Promise Maker? Would Abraham choose to hold onto the answer to his prayers, or would he choose to follow the one to whom he prayed? Would Abraham hold tightly to what he had been given, or cling to the one who both gives and takes away?

"'Don't lay a hand on the boy!' the angel said. 'Do not hurt him in any way, for now I know that you truly fear God. You have not withheld from me even your son, your only son.'" (Genesis 22:12)

We can read this and think, "Phew, I'm glad that's not me!" But this wasn't a one-off ancient challenge. It is presented to us, too. Do we pursue the promises more than we pursue the Promise Maker? Do we value what He gives us more than what He actually is to us? Will we choose to be faithful to He who is faithful?

However inadequate we feel to meet the faithfulness challenge, we should be encouraged that it is He who, *"is able, through his mighty power at work within us, to accomplish infinitely more than we might ask or think. Glory to him in the church and in Christ Jesus through all generations forever and ever! Amen"* (Ephesians 3:20-21).

As Moses knew, *"God is not a man, so he does not lie. He is not human, so he does not change his mind. Has he ever spoken and failed to act? Has he ever promised and not carried it through?"* (Numbers 23:19)

When the source of our faithfulness is He who IS faithful, we can grow in confidence even as we grow in fruitfulness.

As David wrote,

"Your unfailing love, O Lord, is as vast as the heavens; your faithfulness reaches beyond the clouds. Your righteousness is like the mighty mountains, your justice like the ocean depths. You care for people and animals alike, O Lord. How precious is your unfailing love, O God! All humanity finds shelter in the shadow of your wings." (Psalm 36:5-7) and,

"O Lord God of Heaven's Armies! Where is there anyone as mighty as you, O Lord? You are entirely faithful." (Psalm 89:8)

We can be faithful because we are in Him who is faithfulness. He is everything we need to live a faithful life. As Paul wrote to the Corinthians,

"This confirms that what I told you about Christ is true. Now you have every spiritual gift you need as you eagerly wait for the return of our Lord Jesus Christ. He will keep you strong to the end so that you will be free from all blame on the day when our Lord Jesus Christ returns. God will do this, for he is faithful to do what he says, and he has invited you into partnership with his Son, Jesus Christ our Lord." (1 Corinthians 1:6-9)

It is our partnership with Christ, as we remain in Him, that enables His faithfulness to flow through us. This is the beautiful reality that our faithfulness to Him is enabled by His faithfulness to us.

All of us have broken promises at some stage in our lives. Some will have been small with insignificant consequences. However, other promises were perhaps more significant, even covenantal. These promises, when broken, leave devastating wounds in us, and others. The damage often extends from generation to generation. Yet, thank God, He remains faithful to all generations.

Faithfulness as an expression of the fruit of the Spirit is not just about what we can do to be consistent and true, but rather how can we demonstrate the faithfulness of God as we remain rooted in Christ. This is another reason to root firmly into the faithfulness of Christ. In Him there is forgiveness, healing, restoration, grace and hope. In His faithfulness we can be assured that we are loved, accepted and forgiven. Through His faithfulness we can know His healing grace, which can soothe our wounds and soften our scar-tissue. His faithfulness is enough to overcome our un-faithfulness. As John wrote, *"But if we confess our sins to him, he is faithful and just to forgive us our sins and to cleanse us from all wickedness."* (1 John 1:9)

As we draw close to Him, rooted in His truth, remaining obedient, remaining in His faithfulness, there is forgiveness, healing, fresh mercies and hope.

Meditate on this:
"The faithful love of the Lord never ends! His mercies never cease. Great is his faithfulness; his mercies begin afresh each morning. I say to myself, 'The Lord is my inheritance; therefore, I will hope in him!' The Lord is good to those who depend on him, to those who search for him. So it is good to wait quietly for salvation from the Lord. And it is good for people to submit at an early age to the yoke of his discipline." (Lamentations 3:22-27)

Going deeper still:
Today, do you need to repent of any promises you've broken, or

forgive anyone for their broken promises? If so, why not take some time now to talk this through with the Lord in prayer, and even with someone else you trust at some point today?

Let's pray...
Lord, I thank you that throughout history you have been and will be faithful. I thank you that you don't change, but remain true yesterday, today and forever. Lord, will you help me to grow in your faithfulness that I might grow more faithful? Amen.

DAY 36:
STRONGLY GENTLE

*"Come and show me your mercy, as you do for all who love
your name."*
(Psalm 119:132)

Our first child was less than six weeks old and I was not only a
completely inexperienced parent, I was also sleep-deprived and
utterly exhausted. The days seemed easier than the nights, which
were becoming a real challenge to this inexperienced mum. I
wasn't sure if I would ever sleep ever again! I couldn't understand
how my daughter seemed to be able to sleep during the day, but it
would evade her completely at night! I wasn't adapting too quickly
to daytime sleeping, and so was becoming more and more tired.

One night was particularly difficult. I couldn't get my daughter
to settle and I was beginning to lose all sense of calm. As soon as
I put her down and shut my eyes to collapse into sleep, she would
begin crying again, in a repetitive cycle of failed attempts. She
was becoming like a persistent alarm clock that would beep as
soon as I closed my eyes, demanding I wake up. The only trouble
was she had no snooze-button to thump. And thumping was not
really an option!

However, I have to confess that thumping something was
what I really wanted to do. I woke Tim up – not to thump him,
but to ask for help. I literally held our crying daughter over his

sleeping head and then pretended to apologise that we woke him! Even though he would be getting up early to go to work in a few hours, I was at a critical point and intervention was needed. In my tiredness and frustration I needed to use all my strength to be gentle. I needed to contain my strength to match my baby's vulnerability.

Sometimes I think we perceive gentleness as softness, even as weakness. However, I am suggesting that gentleness is true strength. Gentleness will be what causes us to scoop up the crying child and not push them away. Gentleness will come forth when we don't speak those harsh words in anger, but speak words of love. Gentleness appears when we don't write that rude text or turn our back on someone in need.

Jesus is often depicted in artistic impressions of Him with children on His lap or lambs by His feet. They are pictures of a meek gentleness. However, today I want us to look at this in a different way: at the strength of gentleness.

In 1 Kings we read stories that are peppered with brutality as God vindicated His people and His name, sometimes in extreme and violent ways. On one particular occasion the prophet Elijah was caught in a contest with the prophets of Baal to determine who was the true God, Baal or Yahweh. A famine had struck the land and the rains were long removed. So Elijah "competed" with the prophets of Baal to see who had the strongest God. The test was to see which could light a fire! Spoiler alert – Yahweh wins! He always wins. After this, Elijah cleansed the land of the false prophets of Baal by killing them all! God moved, the rains came and the drought was concluded. However, the killing didn't increase Elijah's popularity and Jezebel determined to kill him. All rather brutal and all rather extreme. What happens next though is quite fascinating:

Elijah goes into hiding and starts reminding God of his zealous service, whilst requesting favour and protection.

"'I have zealously served the Lord God Almighty. But the people of Israel have broken their covenant with you, torn down your altars, and killed every one of your prophets. I am the only one left, and now they are trying to kill me, too.' 'Go out and stand before me on the mountain,' the Lord told him. And as Elijah stood there, the Lord passed by, and a mighty windstorm hit the mountain. It was such a terrible blast that the rocks were torn loose, but the Lord was not in the wind. After the wind there was an earthquake, but the Lord was not in the earthquake. And after the earthquake there was a fire, but the Lord was not in the fire. And after the fire there was the sound of a gentle whisper. When Elijah heard it, he wrapped his face in his cloak and went out and stood at the entrance of the cave. And a voice said, 'What are you doing here, Elijah?' He replied again, 'I have zealously served the Lord God Almighty. But the people of Israel have broken their covenant with you, torn down your altars, and killed every one of your prophets. I am the only one left, and now they are trying to kill me, too.' Then the Lord told him, 'Go back the same way you came, and travel to the wilderness of Damascus.'" (1 Kings 19:10-15)

The same God who had allowed massacres and brought about killings; the same God who had lit the altar which had been drenched with water and burned up the sacrifice in a breath; the same God who brought the ferocious rains that ended the drought; this same God who fills the skies and the earth with His presence was, and is able, to contain all His strength and hold himself in a gentle whisper. Out of love for Elijah the Lord contains His power and comes in a gentle whisper.

As Isaiah prophesied, the Lord – because of His love and desire for relationship with His people to be restored – declared,

"Yet for my own sake and for the honour of my name, I will hold back my anger and not wipe you out." (Isaiah 48:9)

Gentleness brings compassion and mercy in a containment of strength that is full of love and nurture. Gentleness holds back that which might crush in order to build up. Gentleness lavishes love and curtails the wild and reckless display of power. Gentleness might express tender-heartedness, meekness and mildness, yet it does so from an awareness of strength in submission.

As we are rooted in Christ who is gentle, so we can grow in gentleness. Paul urged the believers to recognise that because they were in Christ, because of the love they had in Him, they should be gentle in response to each other.

"Always be humble and gentle. Be patient with each other, making allowance for each other's faults because of your love." (Ephesians 4:2)

Meditate on this:
"A gentle answer deflects anger, but harsh words make tempers flare." (Proverbs 15:1)

Going deeper still:
In what ways do you need to hold back your strength to allow gentleness in your words and actions? In what ways can you grow in receiving more from Christ to be able to give away even more?

Let's pray...
Father, I thank you that you are gracious, kind and gentle with me. I thank you that you hold back your anger and you remove my sins from me. I am sorry that I've not always spoken or acted gently. Lord, please fill me again with your Spirit, so that I can grow more and more like you. Amen.

DAY 37:
MARSHMALLOW MOMENTS

———•———

"How can a young person stay pure? By obeying your word."
(Psalm 119:9)

Self-control, or self-discipline, is the ability to stop ourselves from doing something that we might want to do, but which is perhaps not in our best interest, or the best interests of others. Conversely, it enables us to do those things that we may not want to do, but which are in our best interests to do.

Self-control has a wide spectrum of influence, from the person who says no to that second biscuit, to the one who chooses sobriety over drunkenness, or sexual purity over promiscuity. Self-control keeps the dieter on target and the athlete on the training track. It appears in the life of the teenager who, though they love their friends, chooses not to succumb to peer pressure to join in their bad habit of taking mood altering substances. On a personal note, self- discipline is what got me to the gym this morning when I really wanted to stay in bed, and self-control is what I let go of when I shouted at my kids when I got home!

James understood the challenge of self-control when he wrote,

"For if we could control our tongues, we would be perfect and could also control ourselves in every other way. We can make a large horse go wherever we want by means of a small bit in its mouth. And a small rudder makes a huge ship turn wherever the

pilot chooses to go, even though the winds are strong. In the same way, the tongue is a small thing that makes grand speeches. But a tiny spark can set a great forest on fire. And among all the parts of the body, the tongue is a flame of fire. It is a whole world of wickedness, corrupting your entire body. It can set your whole life on fire, for it is set on fire by hell itself." (James 3:2-6)

Speaking for myself, if I'm trying to exercise self-control in my own strength, it's something I don't always achieve and it is certainly easier said than done.

There was a famous scientific experiment held at Stanford University, led by Walter Mischel in the 1960s. Children were sat at a table with a "reward" in front of them, such as a marshmallow or a cookie. They were told they could eat the treat immediately or have two if they waited 15 minutes. The children were then left alone with the one cookie/marshmallow and the test began! The findings were fascinating. Some ate the marshmallow straight away, while others waited in order to get two. Mischel tracked the children's subsequent progress in life, and found that those who delayed gratification went on to live more fulfilled and productive lives. The children who wanted instant gratification were reported to have more issues in later life, such as addictions, or work and relational struggles.

Now before we get disheartened because we've just eaten two cookies and we think our destiny is in crumbs, part of Mischel's conclusion was that self-control can be taught.

Paul would agree. He wrote to Titus encouraging him to,

"Teach the older men to exercise self-control, to be worthy of respect, and to live wisely. They must have sound faith and be filled with love and patience." (Titus 2:2)

Mischel's "marshmallow test" as it became known was videoed and has since been repeated by many others, so there are lots of clips of children trying to resist the treat in front of them. Interestingly, most of the children who kept looking at the marshmallow, touching it and sniffing it, went on to actually taste it. However the children who looked away and tried to think about something else, almost pretending the marshmallow didn't exist, went on to later enjoy two!

This tells us something about how God designed us. What we think about and focus on makes a huge difference in regard to our self-control. For the Christian this can go even further because it is who we focus on that makes the biggest difference of all. When our self-control becomes surrendered to Christ's control we will see significant fruitful growth.

Paul also had a good understanding of the challenges of self-control when he wrote,

"So the trouble is not with the law, for it is spiritual and good. The trouble is with me, for I am all too human, a slave to sin. I don't really understand myself, for I want to do what is right, but I don't do it. Instead, I do what I hate. But if I know that what I am doing is wrong, this shows that I agree that the law is good. So I am not the one doing wrong; it is sin living in me that does it." (Romans 7:14-17)

As Paul writes, the impact on his self-control is not from external pressures as much as that which is within him. Sin! It is the inner self that produces the self-control – or lack of it.

Paul went on to write,

"Those who are dominated by the sinful nature think about sinful things, but those who are controlled by the Holy Spirit think about things that please the Spirit." (Romans 8:5)

The only way to have self-control on the outside is to be filled with Christ-control on the inside. In our own strength we are not strong enough to withstand all the tests that are ahead of us and we can't do things in our own ability to muster self-control. However Christ is more than able. Armed with a profound and complete knowledge of truth He wielded His strength in the face of the enemy and never compromised in sin. It is His strength in battle that enables us to be strong in battle too.

It is because of the Holy Spirit within us that we can have self-control over our bodies as Paul wrote,

"Don't you realise that your body is the temple of the Holy Spirit, who lives in you and was given to you by God? You do not belong to yourself, for God bought you with a high price. So you must honour God with your body." (1 Corinthians 6:19-20)

The Lord really does care about our sexual partners, what we eat and drink, how we look after our bodies and if we allow Christ-control to be our self-control. He does care about what we think, what we say and what we do.

Meditate on this:
"We demolish arguments and every pretension that sets itself up against the knowledge of God, and we take captive every thought to make it obedient to Christ." (2 Corinthians 10:5)

Going deeper still:
In what areas do you struggle the most with regard to self-control? With an accountability partner make a plan today for growing in self-control in this area. Ask this friend, and ask God Himself, to help you.

Let's pray…
Jesus, I choose to submit the control of my life to you. I choose to let you be Lord of my life today. May I live by Christ-control in every thought, word and action today, that through me and in me people will see you. Amen.

DAY 38:
EVERGREEN

———·———

"Oh, that my actions would consistently reflect your decrees!"
(Psalm 119:5)

Recently, I was walking in a beautiful park when I found myself walking alongside a bank of phenomenal rhododendrons. They were beautiful, robust, huge plants with massive flowers. As evergreen plants rhododendrons will always show signs of life with their deep green leaves. Nostalgia flooded in, taking me to a happy place that, to be honest, I didn't know existed. I was reminded of my parents' garden where there had been two huge entwined rhododendrons. It was such an extensive spread, yet there was space within it for my sister and I to easily make a den – a great place to hide and indulge our creative imaginations. Because it was evergreen, there was a year-round possibility of hiding within it, protected from discovery. I don't have the same plants in my garden now, but without doubt, I have a particular preference to those evergreens. We have a few hebes filling our flowerbed, providing an essential back-stop for all the ballgames and protecting our otherwise exposed windows! Evergreens provided my childhood with imagination and creativity and my adulthood with reassurance that my windows won't smash! Such useful plants – all year round!

Ezekiel, a priest in a family line of priests, was prophesying to the God-followers re-gathering after their exile. Having been scattered whilst fleeing persecution they were beginning to return for the rebuilding of the temple and then to rebuild the city wall under Nehemiah's leadership. Celebrating the variety and vibrancy of life that came from being rooted in truth, Ezekiel prophesied about the community transformation that would come as a result.

Mixed with judgement for their sins, Ezekiel's prophecy included revelation of what the Lord desired for His people. To be like trees watered from His sanctuary, rooted and fruitful, with fruit for food and evergreen leaves for healing.

"Fruit trees of all kinds will grow along both sides of the river. The leaves of these trees will never turn brown and fall, and there will always be fruit on their branches. There will be a new crop every month, for they are watered by the river flowing from the Temple. The fruit will be for food and the leaves for healing." (Ezekiel 47:12)

Ezekiel envisioned people rooted in their God, bearing fruit – enough fruit to share and even more to give away; a constantly replenished abundant life. But throughout their lives there would be the constant presence of evergreen leaves. They wouldn't turn brown or fall to the ground, they would be mature, reliable and, according to Ezekiel, have healing properties.

Remember when we discussed how Jesus wants us to be disciples who are distinct? The salt in society, bringing qualities of preservation and healing; enhancing the flavour and fertilising to encourage the most growth. Here too, we are encouraged that our evergreen qualities are to make a difference to those around us, and specifically to bring healing. It is the people of God who are to be fruitful and who bring healing to all those around.

Our fruitfulness is not simply to make us look good and feel good. Our fruitfulness is to be a sign for others to see. An evergreen, ever salty, lit-up sign that points to Jesus. A fruitfulness that has leaves for healing, much like salt's medicinal qualities.

There is a well-known, often adapted prayer of St Francis of Assisi, written back in the 13th Century. St Francis understood what his evergreen qualities were – not for himself, but rather to make a difference for others.

Lord, make me an instrument of thy peace.
Where there is hatred, let me sow love;
Where there is injury, pardon;
Where there is doubt, faith;
Where there is despair, hope;
Where there is darkness, light;
Where there is sadness, joy.

O Divine Master, grant that I may not so much seek
To be consoled as to console,
To be understood as to understand,
To be loved as to love;
For it is in giving that we receive;
It is in pardoning that we are pardoned;
It is in dying to self that we are born to eternal life.

In the same encouragement to His disciples to be salty, Jesus also said, *"You are the light of the world – like a city on a hilltop that cannot be hidden. No one lights a lamp and then puts it under a basket. Instead, a lamp is placed on a stand, where it gives light to everyone in the house. In the same way, let your good deeds shine out for all to see, so that everyone will praise your heavenly Father"* (Matthew 5:14-16).

For many years, one of our neighbouring houses had a large tree in its front garden. It had been there for over forty years, having been planted by the previous owners. However, the tree had grown much taller than the house and our new neighbours decided it needed to be removed. Something surprising happened though, once the tree was removed. A few of our friends missed our house when they were coming to visit, because the big landmark they were used to seeing had gone. Like our neighbours' tree, we are meant to be signposts for people to find Jesus. When they see us they should be able to see Him. Our evergreen, lit up, consistent sign-post lifestyles should show people Jesus.

At the moment we have a weird electrical challenge in our home. A mysterious problem that we've not sourced yet, which results in our kitchen lights being inconsistent when they are first turned on. Even more bizarrely, the other day I simply opened the microwave door and that was enough for the kitchen lights to go out! We're not talking a fuse issue, but an inconsistency to supply light to the room!

This stands out as unusual because we expect our kitchen lights to be consistent. In the same way, we long to live lives of consistency. Inconsistency is not enough for us, nor is it enough for our community. Our communities deserve the best. An evergreen plant is like an everlasting light and is consistent and reliable. It is not good enough for the lights to suddenly go out when an appliance is used. Pressure is not a reason to stop shining, as it is not in our strength but the Lord's that we even shine.

So through the prophet Ezekiel, and through the words of Jesus, we are encouraged to stand out, shine out, and be a signpost and a beacon of hope. Let those trying to find Jesus use you as the landmark that they can't miss. The consistent, reliable, evergreen plant.

Mediate on this:

"Be careful to live properly among your unbelieving neighbours. Then even if they accuse you of doing wrong, they will see your honourable behaviour, and they will give honour to God when he judges the world." (1 Peter 2:12)

Going deeper still:

In what ways could you be more consistent, evergreen, for your neighbours, colleagues, family, and friends to be able to see Jesus in you? What needs to change for this to happen?

Let's pray...

Lord, I thank you for the reminder that evergreen plants really are evergreen all year. Thank you that you long for me to be consistent and reliable in my witness and walk with you. Lord, please help me to root into your truth even more – so that my neighbours will see you in me and come to know you. Amen.

DAY 39:
STANDING BACK

———•———

"Let me live so I can praise you, and may your regulations help me."
(Psalm 119:175)

Today, as we prepare to continue our walk of fruitfulness by first remaining in Christ we are going to consider for just a few moments what happens when the Gardener steps back.

If you've ever watched an expert gardener planting out a flowerbed, you will see them bent over, focused closely, working in detail most of the time. However, to get a better perspective they will regularly step back and cast their eyes over the full flowerbed, making sure that their detailed work fits in with the bigger picture.

In Chronicles we read the story of King Hezekiah. He was a king who wanted to do what was right by the Lord and so remained in the Lord, which meant as a result he was fruitful and successful in all he did. Apparently,

"King Hezekiah handled the distribution throughout all Judah, doing what was pleasing and good in the sight of the Lord his God. In all that he did in the service of the Temple of God and in his efforts to follow God's laws and commands, Hezekiah sought his God wholeheartedly. As a result, he was very successful." (2 Chronicles 31:20-21)

Cleaning up after his father's wicked reign Hezekiah loved the

Lord and His commandments.

"He remained faithful to the Lord in everything, and he carefully obeyed all the commands the Lord had given Moses." (2 Kings 18:6)

However, Hezekiah knew what it was for the Lord to step back to observe. Hezekiah's reign took an unfortunate turn when,

"About that time Hezekiah became deathly ill. He prayed to the Lord, who healed him and gave him a miraculous sign. But Hezekiah did not respond appropriately to the kindness shown him, and he became proud. So the Lord's anger came against him and against Judah and Jerusalem. Then Hezekiah humbled himself and repented of his pride, as did the people of Jerusalem. So the Lord's anger did not fall on them during Hezekiah's lifetime." (2 Chronicles 32:24-26)

Hezekiah's leadership impacted those around him to such an extent that when he repented so did they. This in turn impacted the Lord's blessings experienced by them all. The extent to which Hezekiah remained faithful to the Lord determined the blessing and favour that fell on those around him.

When our lives remain in Christ, they bear much more fruit than we ever could on our own. This is the evergreen nature of our identities. When Hezekiah gave into his sinful nature he harvested fruit after this kind – and pride and judgement was the result, both on him and the nation. When he humbled himself and remained in God, the fruit from his life was the Holy Spirit kind, and favour returned to the community too.

Fascinatingly though, the story still doesn't end there. Remember the idea of the gardener working in the detail and then he stepping back to observe?

"However, when ambassadors arrived from Babylon to ask about the remarkable events that had taken place in the land, God withdrew from Hezekiah in order to test him and to see what was

really in his heart." (2 Chronicles 32:31)

The Lord wanted to see what was in Hezekiah's heart, or rather who was in his heart, and so He stepped back and withdrew. Hezekiah's fruitfulness came from the fact that he remained in the Lord, rooted in truth and pursuing right living. His fruitfulness was not down to him being a good or clever person, but rather a rooted and fruitful person. Yet, the Lord removed Himself to see if Hezekiah drew praise to himself about the remarkable events or brought glory to the Lord.

Whether now, or in the days to come, there are going to be occasions when it will feel like the Lord has removed Himself a little from you, as if He is stepping back. He is still nearby. He is still loving and still wanting to display His glory in and through you. But He will be looking to see what (or who) is in your heart. Stay. Remain. Be rooted in His truth. Don't be scared of the heat or draw strength from yourself. Don't draw praise to yourself either, but bring pleasure to the Father. God is omnipresent (everywhere) and has promised to never leave nor forsake you, so He has not gone but He might step back. He steps back to allow you to display His glory – to show your heart is remaining in Him.

Remember, we are children of the Living God because of who He is not because of what we get. There will be times ahead when things might not go as you would expect, or even as you would have chosen. Remain. Don't give up.

As Isaiah reminds us,

"'My thoughts are nothing like your thoughts,' says the Lord. 'And my ways are far beyond anything you could imagine. For just as the heavens are higher than the earth, so my ways are higher than your ways and my thoughts higher than your thoughts.'" (Isaiah 55:8-9)

In the Garden of Eden, Adam and Eve walked in perfect harmony with their Creator; blessed in relationship with the

Almighty. Yet they took their eyes off their relationship with God when Eve first became distracted by the beauty of the fruit from the one tree which was forbidden.

"She saw that the tree was beautiful and its fruit looked delicious, and she wanted the wisdom it would give her. So she took some of the fruit and ate it. Then she gave some to her husband, who was with her, and he ate it, too. At that moment their eyes were opened, and they suddenly felt shame at their nakedness." (Genesis 3:6-7)

Eve and Adam took their eyes off the Father and focused on the fruit. As a result the relationship with the Father was broken.

When we have a Christ-centric focus we grow fruitful, but when we have a fruit-centric focus we do not grow Christ like. The difference is in the focus. Check your attitude and do not be fearful if the Lord stands back for a moment. Keep your focus on Christ and remain in Him.

Meditate on this:
"And now, dear brothers and sisters, one final thing. Fix your thoughts on what is true, and honourable, and right, and pure, and lovely, and admirable. Think about things that are excellent and worthy of praise. Keep putting into practice all you learned and received from me – everything you heard from me and saw me doing. Then the God of peace will be with you." (Philippians 4:8-9)

Going deeper still:
In what ways can you check your focus and make sure your eyes are on who Christ is as you remain in Him?

Let's pray...
Lord, I thank you that you care so much about the detail of my life and everyone's life. Lord, I choose to trust you. I know that you

are in the detail of my life, even if it feels like you've stepped back for a moment. Jesus please keep me remaining in you that you will be remaining in me. Amen.

DAY 40:
EXPECT MORE

—·—

"I rejoice in your word like one who discovers a great treasure."
(Psalm 119:162)

Well, we are nearly at the end of this part of our journey, which of course is just the beginning of the next stage! Forty days of exploring what it is to be rooted, remaining in Christ (who is the vine) cared for by the Father (who is the Gardener) so that we, (the branches) might bear fruit. As Jesus said,

"Yes, I am the vine; you are the branches. Those who remain in me, and I in them, will produce much fruit. For apart from me you can do nothing. Anyone who does not remain in me is thrown away like a useless branch and withers. Such branches are gathered into a pile to be burned. But if you remain in me and my words remain in you, you may ask for anything you want, and it will be granted! When you produce much fruit, you are my true disciples. This brings great glory to my Father." (John 15:5-8)

We will be known as Jesus' disciples by our fruitfulness.

After Jesus' resurrection He spent some time catching up again with His friends and family. Not just for a jolly, but to help them understand what He'd been saying all along! Helping them to realise who He really was, and is. Then just prior to His ascension Jesus gave His disciples the Great Commission:

"Jesus came and told his disciples, 'I have been given all authority

in heaven and on earth. *Therefore, go and make disciples of all the nations, baptising them in the name of the Father and the Son and the Holy Spirit. Teach these new disciples to obey all the commands I have given you. And be sure of this: I am with you always, even to the end of the age."* (Matthew 28:18-20)

All Christ-followers have the same primary calling in life, so whilst our secondary callings are unique to each of us, our primary calling is universally the same. We are called to be disciples who make disciples. We are called to be fruitful and that fruit is to have seed in it!

Our lives are designed for Kingdom transformation and to spread gospel seeds for new life everywhere we are planted, yet not limited to where we are planted! We are to have seeds with wings! Much like the sycamore seeds, or the Sequoia seeds we talked about earlier, our influence in the times in which we're living can go way beyond our physical proximity. Our fruit can go further and the seeds within can go further still.

I heard this phrase once, "you can tell how many seeds are within an apple, but you can't tell how many apples are within a seed". This is the Kingdom of God – that we will bear fruit for the Father's glory and that we will make disciples who go on to make disciples.

The prophet Ezekiel spoke of fruitfulness in words that are now familiar to us, but we are going to reflect just one more time on them together.

"Fruit trees of all kinds will grow along both sides of the river. The leaves of these trees will never turn brown and fall, and there will always be fruit on their branches. There will be a new crop every month, for they are watered by the river flowing from the Temple. The fruit will be for food and the leaves for healing." (Ezekiel 47:12)

Ezekiel prophesied that there would not only always be fruit on the branches, but there would be new fruit every month. Always fruitful and still new fruit coming. Always fruitful and yet more to be expected.

My friend, whilst we must not become fruit-centric but remain as Christ-centric followers, we should, however, confidently expect more fruit! As we remain in Christ we will grow in our understanding and knowledge of Him and we will grow in our experience of Him. We will know Him as true Love and so grow more in love and show more of His love to others. As we remain in Him we will know Him as Joy. He is our joy and He will be our strength to remain, to keep pursuing.

As we remain in Him so we will meet Him as Peace, know Him as Patience, discover Him as Kindness, see Him as Goodness. We will understand Him as Faithfulness and experience Him as Gentleness and we will welcome Him as Self-Control.

In Him we will discover who He really is and then we will discover all these expressions of fruitfulness coming in our lives. As we grow in Him so we will make disciples who turn away from hate and know love, and who turn their anxious thoughts to the Lord in prayer and know peace. We will make disciples who grow in patience, kindness, goodness, faithfulness, gentleness and self-control.

You see, we are to be fruitful with seed. As we make disciples, we will be making them after our own kind which is of Jesus' kind.

One hugely encouraging and sometimes hugely daunting responsibility that comes with parenting is that we can create and raise a "mini-me"! We raise children who copy our behaviour and mannerisms, who capture our attitudes and our preferences. That's all encouraging if they are copying and emulating the best parts of ourselves. However, it is always a scary wake-up call when they pick up on our weaknesses! As followers of Christ, remaining in Him and bearing fruit, we are not designed to create a "mini-me", but rather we are designed to be, and invited to create, many "mini-Hims"! We are to be children who carry the Father's heart and love like He loves; who carry His eyes and sees like He sees; and who have His seed and bear fruit after His own kind.

Remember when the Father took Abram outside and said to him, *"Look up into the sky and count the stars if you can. That's how many descendants you will have!"* (Genesis 15:5)?

Well, as you remain in Jesus, a similar command and blessing comes to you. That whatever your age you will have a heart like a grandparent to expect fruitfulness with seeds in for further fruitfulness for generations after generations.

Furthermore, you can expect more. Expect the Lord to do new things and show you new things as you get to know Him better and better.

Meditate on this:

"Now may the God of peace – who brought up from the dead our Lord Jesus, the great Shepherd of the sheep, and ratified an eternal covenant with his blood – may he equip you with all you need for doing his will. May he produce in you, through the power of Jesus Christ, every good thing that is pleasing to him. All glory to him forever and ever! Amen." (Hebrews 13:20-21)

Going deeper still:

What steps and accountability can you put in place to continue growing in Him with faith, so that you continue to bear fruit, new fruit and more fruit, in Him? If you don't have an accountability partner already, I encourage you to get one. And if you are not rooted in a local church, I urge you to join one. What reading plan or devotional journey are you going to go on now?

Let's pray…

Lord, may I love you more, see you more, and follow you more. Lord, please give me a heart for the generations of disciples that you want to raise through me. May I remain in you, that your fruitfulness will come through me and that you will produce in me and through me after your own kind. For the Father's glory and pleasure. Amen.

About the Author

Helen is the Executive Minister of Wellspring Church, a multi-ethnic, multi-congregational church family based in Watford, just outside London. She and her husband have lived in the Watford area since the mid-1990s and have been leading Wellspring Church together since 1998.

Drawing from a range of experience in the hotel business, overseas mission, Christian youth work and raising three enthusiastic children, Helen has become a strategic leader and an inspiring communicator who loves connecting people to the liberating truth of God's word. She enjoys time with her family, good books, regular exercise and holidays.

Follow her on Twitter: @HelenRoberts_1